GET TO KNOW A CEO

Create Community and Unite Your Team while Enhancing Communication Skills

EVA MARIA HAMILTON

Award Winning
Co-Founder and Co-CEO
TESTLAUNCHER Inc.

Dedicated with love to my family,

especially my husband, Jason;

our daughters, Michelina and Angelina;

my parents, Bob and Lina;

and my brother, Bill.

Thank you to everyone who gave me their permission to use my photos from their establishments, etc. It was very much appreciated.

Thank you to Jason, Michelina, and Angelina for all your contributions. Your help made this book everything I imagined, and more.

And thank you to the Launchers who offered their Welcome To Watercooler Wednesday testimonials. And to every Launcher who helped make, and continue to make, Welcome To Watercooler Wednesday a success at TestLauncher.

WELCOME TO WATERCOOLER WEDNESDAY!

GET TO KNOW A CEO AS YOU EMBARK ON A JOURNEY TO CREATE COMMUNITY, STRENGTHEN YOUR TEAM, AND ENRICH YOUR COMPANY CULTURE

OVER 5 YEARS OF TOPICS TO START EACH WEEKLY DISCUSSION

PERFECT FOR REMOTE TEAM BUILDING AND/OR SOCIAL MEDIA ENGAGEMENT

www.LilacLanePublishing.com
ISBN: 978-1-0689907-7-9

In 2015, my Co-Founder and Co-CEO, Jason Hamilton, and I, began TestLauncher as a remote business. Back then, before the Covid-19 pandemic, remote work was much more rare, and an entirely remote company was even more so. Thankfully, it proved to offer our employees, and ourselves, what we had always hoped for: a better quality of life.

However, working as a remote team has its own set of challenges, and the one we're going to tackle in this book is how to improve your team's communication skills and boost their ability to socialize with one another through what we call, Welcome To Watercooler Wednesday. This tool will also enable you to get to know your team on a more personal level, with minimal intrusion.

And whether or not you're the CEO of a company, you are still the CEO of your own life, and hence as the title of this book promises, not only will you get to know more about me by reading this book, you will also get to know a lot more about yourself.

So even if you don't run a company, the great thing about this book is that it lends itself perfectly to social media and community building, where you can use its over 5 years of weekly questions to engage with those in your channels.

However, if you do manage a company, this book is a win-win because you can create an internal Welcome To Watercooler Wednesday for your employees, and an external Welcome To Watercooler Wednesday to connect with customers, friends, and future clients.

For simplicity's sake though, this book will discuss TestLauncher's internal Welcome To Watercooler Wednesday, and leave you to extrapolate all the positive outcomes of building and strengthening your community through an external Welcome To Watercooler Wednesday.

So let's get started. At TestLauncher, much like what you encounter on social media, our employees span the globe. As such, some members of our team work at different hours, and the Welcome To Watercooler Wednesday format gives everyone a space to talk whenever they are able to, instead of in real time.

This space also allows them the opportunity to talk about things outside of their work. We also have other areas, such as our Launcher Lounge, where our employees, known as Launchers, can talk about anything they wish, whenever they wish. And an Animal Area, because our employees have an affinity for animals and enjoy an area to post photos and tell stories about their pets or the animals they encounter in nature.

These all blend together, among other tools and initiatives, to generate a sense of unity, which can be hard to establish when people work from different time zones across the world. And yet they are essential.

When leading remote workers, it's imperative to find ways to create team cohesion so employees do not feel disengaged or isolated.

And with remote work here to stay, it's essential to address the issue of team building to attract the best employees, decrease employee turnover, and increase employee happiness, which in turn will have a positive effect company-wide.

So let's jump into the fundamentals of Welcome To Watercooler Wednesday.

Welcome To Watercooler Wednesday is a place where you can consistently model the professional soft skills you expect from your employees. For instance, if your company prides itself on being cooperative and friendly, then that is exactly how your Welcome To Watercooler Wednesday posts should read, and how you should respond to each employee who comments.

Use Welcome To Watercooler Wednesday to model effective communication, good interpersonal skills, enthusiasm, approachability, etc. Use it as yet another tool which reinforces and sets the tone for your business. That being said, always be on the lookout to combat negativity, and never allow anyone to belittle, or harass someone, even jokingly. Keep it upbeat, amiable, interesting, and hopefully inspiring. Have fun with it!

The positivity your employees feel will extend to other areas of their lives, and to the work they do. And as everyone shares their thoughts and personal experiences this will bring them closer together and foster a supportive environment. This collaborative atmosphere will strengthen your workplace. Your employees will be working with their friends, not merely just co-workers, or worse, strangers.

So let's get to work on building, or enhancing, a great work culture through the use of Welcome To Watercooler Wednesday.

First, decide on the best person, or people, to run Welcome To Watercooler Wednesday. At TestLauncher, I do it, because it offers me the opportunity to get to know our employees on a more personal level.

However, you can always hire us to implement Welcome To Watercooler Wednesday for you. Then, along with your team, you can simply answer the question(s) every week while still providing an amazing opportunity to unify your team. For more information, please visit: www.WelcomeToWatercoolerWednesday.com

At TestLauncher, Welcome To Watercooler Wednesday is on Slack. However, we have run it on different platforms, and can do that for you, as well.

Welcome To Watercooler Wednesday is not obligatory at TestLauncher. Our employees are encouraged to participate, but they're not required to, just like socializing with colleagues would be at a physical location. We want to make sure it's a fun spot. Somewhere they want to go and chat.

Nevertheless, you will notice differences among your employees. Some may be very involved in Welcome To Watercooler Wednesday and will reap the benefits. Others however, for a multitude of reasons, may only comment on rare occasions. However, don't be insulted or discouraged. Some may not post, but may in fact read the posts, along with everyone's answers, and hence still feel part of a terrific team.

And I will show you the validation I received. After I wrote this book, I told our team about it, and asked if any of them would like to contribute. You will see from their testimonials in the next section that some of their quotes mirror what I just said.

However, one way to increase employee participation, without having to call them out on it, is through Welcome To Watercooler Wednesday's sheer variety of topics. One of the topics will hopefully pique their interest at some point and they will engage.

Another way to increase your employees' involvement, and give them more ownership of Welcome To Watercooler Wednesday, is to ask them to contribute topics and questions for Welcome To Watercooler Wednesday. In this book however, we didn't use any of our employees' questions, or any of their answers. To see those, you must be an employee of TestLauncher, because Welcome To Watercooler Wednesday is a safe place for our employees to hang out and share their lives with one another. But you can create that same safe haven within your company. It doesn't take long, nor does it take much time for your employees to respond, because just like at a physical water cooler in an office, employees wouldn't be standing around there talking all day.

So let's dissect what goes into each Welcome To Watercooler Wednesday post.

To add interest, every Welcome To Watercooler Wednesday begins with a photo about that week's topic. You can add videos if you wish. I try to use media from my own life to make each post more personable. In the event that isn't possible, I turn to Canva or some other source. For instance, I took the photo for the cover of this book while in California, but I changed the birds at home when designing it in Adobe Photoshop.

However, please be cognizant of applicable copyright laws. On your own company forum copyright laws aren't as strict and you have more leeway, just like on social media. However, things differ from country to country, and company to company, so please do your own due diligence.

Next, I write the greeting, which is always along the lines of, Welcome To Watercooler Wednesday!

Then, I usually comment on whatever we talked about the previous week, before we get into that week's topic.

If it's a question from an employee, I always give that employee kudos and thank them for their question(s), because their initiative is something we value, hence, we always want to commend and encourage it.

I also answer the question(s) myself, as you'll see later.

After employees begin answering the question(s), I comment on every employees' answer to ensure they feel heard and valued. I never pick and choose which answers I comment on because that would inevitably cause hard feelings, which is the exact opposite of what we're striving for.

In response to employees' comments, ask questions to stimulate more conversation. And try to promote an environment where employees respond and talk to one another. This is especially important between employees who may have little or no interaction during the course of their work.

And remember, this is a place to model company culture, so always be courteous, kind, etc. And if an employee is rude, offensive, uses inappropriate language, or whatever your company deems to be unacceptable, deal with such behaviour immediately. We've never really had any issues at TestLauncher, and I hope you don't either.

Welcome To Watercooler Wednesday is for everyone within the company to get to know one another, and that should include upper management. Allow employees access to everyone, especially you. Be sincere. Remember, people like working with their friends much more than working with people they hardly know.

So what types of questions should you ask?

Let's start with what you shouldn't ask.

Stay away from anything controversial. You do not want your employees arguing. You don't want anyone being upset by what they've read. And be mindful not to alienate employees. For instance, if some of your employees have children, keep in mind that others do not, and hence, avoid continuously talking about parenting.

At TestLauncher, our employees work from all over the world, they're each individuals, they range in age, live in different cultures, come from diverse backgrounds, and hence they each have their own unique perspectives. Respect this. Speak to this. Celebrate this!

My questions are laid out for you to copy, however if you create your own questions here are some tips: Consider varying the length of your questions, and your posts, to add interest. You don't want the questions to appear the same week after week. Monotony is not your friend. And let your personality shine. I always try to add humour if I can. ☺

Now on to the questions.

I've divided this book into five years, with each year subdivided by month. In each month, I've included five weeks of questions, because depending on the year there may be five Wednesdays in that month.

But, since there are only fifty-two weeks in a year, and your company most likely takes holidays, the sixty posts per year will result in many leftover questions. That's why I've included a box to check off which posts you've used, and a line for you to write in the date you used them.

However, you may prefer to keep track by downloading the list from the Welcome To Watercooler Wednesday website: www.WelcomeToWatercoolerWednesday.com/Books.

And remember, you don't need to use the questions in order. Just keep track so you can clearly see what you have and haven't used, and when you used them.

This record keeping is also important depending on your employee retention rate. For instance, you may be able to go back and reuse some posts in later years, or tweak them to be like new again. Also, there are lots of posts that can be used year after year, such as having your employees share their plans for the new year. And there are questions that can be used every season, such as having your employees share a photo they've recently taken.

And that brings me to my next point, depending on how often you hire new employees, every once in a while you may need to invite your employees to send you their questions for Welcome To Watercooler Wednesday. You may also need to reiterate the guidelines and purpose of Welcome To Watercooler Wednesday so everyone is on the same page.

Now for the fun stuff: Topics to get your employees talking.

You could run a search for questions that would bring back tons of results, but the 300 days of questions in this book have all been curated for a professional, business environment. And the vast majority have already been used at TestLauncher.

As you read through my questions, they will inevitably spark your creativity, and you'll create your own questions. Hence the need to include space in the margins of each page for you to jot down your ideas and answers to the questions.

You will also notice that I didn't include any questions in this book that were time sensitive, because that would make this book obsolete ridiculously fast. But please, remember to ask your employees questions about things that are relevant to the times, such as significant news events, big sporting events, movie premieres, award shows, major weather events, and so on.

You can also run with themes for a month or longer. For instance, as you'll see, we once spent a summer talking about how our employees' gardening was progressing on every last Wednesday of the month.

Find out your employees' interests and ask questions about them. For instance, if you know you have employees who love to cook, ask them to share recipes, or photos of what they've created in the kitchen.

Other ideas for making up your own Welcome To Watercooler Wednesday topics: You can always use whatever national day, week, or month it is. For instance, February 1st is National Dark Chocolate Day. Yum! Who wouldn't want to talk about chocolate?

The first full week in January is National Hunt for Happiness Week. That lends itself to tons of topics, from sharing quotes and stories to helpful advice.

And did you know that January is National Soup Month? That's a good lead-in to discuss whether your employees like soup, what their most or least favourite types of soup are, if they enjoy cooking their own soup from scratch, or prefer bought soup, if they have any fond memories of eating soup, etc.

Whatever you decide, good luck on your journey to create community, and establish a happier, more unified team, with better communication skills.

And **Welcome To Watercooler Wednesday!**

Welcome To Watercooler Wednesday Testimonials

"I look forward to Watercooler Wednesday. Brain teasers, favourite foods, best vacations, people who inspire; the topics presented each week are varied and always interesting. Watercooler Wednesday creates a space - like a virtual break room - where we can drop in and connect with our teammates. A place in our busy week to play, to converse and to share. Watercooler Wednesday contributes to the culture we are building at TestLauncher."
Mike Gerrie - Ontario, Canada

"I love reading Watercooler Wednesday every week. While I don't always contribute, I love reading the contributions of my teammates each week. It allows us to share a side of us we don't always get to talk about in team meetings or correspondence. Working remotely has many benefits, but one of the challenges is the lack of a real, cohesive community among your team members. Some companies make up for this with weekly calls or live events, but just having a weekly discussion around an interesting topic does so much to remind us all that we each have a life we've been living and come from many diverse, interesting backgrounds."
Harry Gillen - Puerto Rico

"What I love most about Watercooler Wednesday is how it breaks the monotony of the workweek and brings a sense of community to our work. It's not just about discussing work related topics, it's about connecting on a personal level, sharing experiences, and getting to know each other beyond our jobs. It allows us to bring our own unique perspectives to the table and encourages creativity and open mindedness since we are from all over the world. As for my favorite types of questions, I particularly enjoy the ones that spark debates or prompt us to think outside the box and obviously about our pets and music!"
Lucas Castagnola - Argentina

"Watercooler Wednesday is awesome! It's a way for us to connect, even though we're working remotely. I enjoy reading it and sometimes contribute. It's fun and helps us feel like a team, even from afar."
Yogita Lad - United Kingdom

"It's an essential chance for us to connect and understand one another better. The varied topics provide a virtual space where we can engage, share, and strengthen our TestLauncher culture. While I may not always contribute, I enjoy reading about my teammates' experiences. Watercooler Wednesday fosters connection in our remote environment and highlights the diversity within our team."
Nina Margulian - Alberta, Canada

"I enjoy seeing posts in Watercooler Wednesday
because it helps me learn more about my fellow
teammates at TestLauncher. I enjoy seeing
pets, info about different cultures, sights,
and food. It is really a great way to stay
connected, especially since we work remotely
and live in different countries."
Katz Rosalina - Philippines

"I am always looking forward to Watercooler
Wednesday! Being a 'people person' I was a bit
anxious to start a remote job as communication
with colleagues and teams played an important
role in my office life. It was a big relief to
learn we have WCW where my colleagues discuss
a variety of topics and have a good laugh
sometimes. I really enjoy spending time here
with regular contributors and encourage my
other coworkers to put away their hesitation
and share their thoughts and opinions.
Watercooler Wednesday is great fun!"
Olesya Shpotyuk – Manitoba, Canada

"I love to see the chat…Always good to see the
ingenious slogans for each week. It brings me
closer to my coworkers because…working
remotely is not a very social way to know them
if you don't have these kinds of spaces.
Thanks for bringing us closer together!"
Hernan Szulanski - Argentina

"In the virtual halls of TestLauncher, Watercooler Wednesday is our communal hearth. Here, we exchange pieces of our world, from the whimsy of our pets to the wonders of our locales, fostering a sense of unity in our distributed team."
Erica Gregory - Newfoundland, Canada

"At the beginning (almost three years ago), I didn't even know what Watercooler Wednesday actually was. To be honest, I was so busy with the first customer I was assigned to, and with the learning curve to go through, that I didn't really care about it. After a while, though, due to the notifications I was receiving by email (thanks to the contributions made by my colleagues) I started being curious about it. So, my current status would be:
- Reading other people's contributions: often;
- Contributing myself: every now and then;
- Enjoying the initiative: always!
All in all, thank you, Eva!"
Ileana Belfiore - Spain

"I love reading Watercooler Wednesday, whether I contribute or not. It's a great way to connect on a personal level with our widespread team. I especially enjoy the food conversations and seeing different dishes from around the world."
Catrina McGregor - New Zealand

"I like the way this brings us together in a non-tester way. I don't usually participate, but I do check on the Watercooler fairly often to see what is going on and read the interesting topics and comments."
Dianne Mead – Ontario, Canada

"Prior to joining TestLauncher in 2018, I had about 10 years of remote work experience on various teams and diverse projects -- but as many others have already mentioned, there wasn't the sense of knowing my teammates in a social or non-work-related community. Watercooler Wednesday brings us all together and while I don't always have a contribution to make every week, I do read everyone's comments and really enjoy the time we get to spend learning about one another. It is by far, one of the things I thoroughly look forward to every week!"
Anne-Marie Short – Newfoundland, Canada

YEAR 1

JANUARY

☐ **#1 Date**_____

Welcome to Watercooler Wednesday!

And Welcome to a New Year!

How were your holidays? Our holidays were really nice and relaxing. We will definitely remember them as peaceful. Everything just went so smooth and perfect. It was great. Lots of fun. And the new year was here before we knew it. A new year full of potential, new things to discover, and new Welcome To Watercooler Wednesday fun! So let's get started!

If you had to pick one new thing to do, or try, in the new year what would it be?

I'd like to try out a new food. And I'm sure I'll have lots of options to choose from. ☺ Perhaps, shepherd's pie? I've never tasted that. Have you? Is it good? (Note: I have now tried it, and it's fantastic! I should never have waited so long. I wonder what else I'm missing out on? Tamales? Any other suggestions?)

☐ **#2 Date**_____

It's Wednesday! Time to gather around the Water Cooler!

At TestLauncher, besides being awesome at testing, making our customers happy is of the utmost importance. So this week I thought we'd talk about customer service, and share our experiences, so we can all reflect on what makes for truly great customer service.

I just recently had a zipper fixed on one of my coats and although they did a good job, I had ordered a two-way zipper and they put on a regular zipper. The owner realized the mistake and was adamant I allow them to give me what we had agreed upon. That took longer, but I was happy with the end result. Would I go back? Yes.

Now that's customer service on a small scale. Here's an example of it from a huge retailer. A month or so after I purchased several items online, I received an email informing me that apparently the company had made an error and were now giving me my entire order free! I hadn't even noticed the mistake. They just fixed it! And I really wish I'd purchased more! ☺

I have so many more examples, but I think we'd all agree that it's wonderful to have a problem solved or a question answered in a friendly, courteous manner.

As for bad customer service, I would hate to be talked down to, ignored, blamed, or left to fall through the cracks. So what experiences have you had with customer service?

☐ **#3 Date**_____

Welcome to another Watercooler Wednesday!

We've been having some wacky weather here in Southern Ontario, Canada.

So today, since we're from all over the world, I thought we'd talk about the weather everyone's experiencing!

It's winter here, and this weekend, we had a snowstorm that dumped around 40cm of snow. By the end of the weekend, and into the beginning of this week, we were out in temperatures of -12°C/10°F with a wind chill of -21.5°C/-7°F.

Today, the temperature is supposed to rise to 3°C/37°F with a wind chill that will make it feel like -3°C/27°F and bring some freezing rain or rain. Then tomorrow our temperatures will plummet again.

How is your weather treating you?

☐ **#4 Date**_____

Welcome to Watercooler Wednesday!

Last week we talked about weather. If you can believe it, today in Southern Ontario, we're expecting it to feel like -35°C/-31°F! So I thought we'd talk about movies today. You know, something fun to do indoors when it's freezing cold or boiling hot outside. ☺

It would be impossible for me to name my favourite movie, so I'm not even going to try. I would need at least a top 100 list. ☺

Can you name your favourite movie? If not, how about your favourite genre?

I think it'll be fun to see how many of us love the same types of movies, if not the same ones!

I would say I gravitate toward comedies. How about you?

☐ **#5 Date**_____

Welcome to Watercooler Wednesday!

What is your astrological sign?

Aries, Taurus, Gemini, Cancer, Leo, Virgo, Libra, Scorpio, Sagittarius, Capricorn, Aquarius, or Pisces?

Do you think astrology is accurate and your sign describes you?

My astrological sign is Cancer, and I really wish it had a different name. Hence, I like being referred to as a Moonchild much better.

As for it describing me, I'm not completely sold on that idea, although when you factor in other details, such as time of birth and birthplace, those add more to the equation than the more commonly known belief that everyone born within the same month are identical.

Perhaps those of you who esteem astrology can offer your insight?

FEBRUARY

☐ **#6 Date**_____

It's Watercooler Wednesday! Hope everyone is having a great day!

Can you believe it's February already? I can't. So today, I thought we'd talk about quotes that inspire, encourage, and/or motivate us. I love quotes, but I'll limit myself to three. ☺ I can't wait to read yours!

"Success means doing the best we can with what we have. Success is the doing, not the getting; in the trying, not the triumph. Success is a personal standard, reaching for the highest that is in us, becoming all that we can be." -Zig Ziglar

"Staying positive does not mean that things will turn out okay. Rather it is knowing that you will be okay no matter how things turn out." -Unknown Author

"When I was 5 years old, my mother always told me that happiness was the key to life. When I went to school, they asked me what I wanted to be when I grew up. I wrote down 'happy'. They told me I didn't understand the assignment, and I told them they didn't understand life." -John Lennon

☐ **#7 Date**_____

It's Watercooler Wednesday!

How's everyone's day going?

Hopefully well!

Want to step into the past?

What was the first pet you ever owned?

How old were you when you got him/her?

Please share anything and everything about your sweet pet.

I was about four years old when we got a green budgie/parakeet. He was social and lived quite a long time: 8 years! The house was never quiet with his joyful chirping. ☺

☐ **#8 Date**_____

Welcome to Watercooler Wednesday!

Let's talk about pizza!

If there's anyone here who doesn't like pizza, please feel free to share what you don't like about it.

For everyone else, how would you design your perfect pizza? What toppings are your favourite? Which ones do you dislike?

I usually enjoy my pizza pretty simple with cheese and pepperoni, although I do like green olives, mushrooms, and/or green peppers. What's most important to me is that the crust isn't hard or burnt.

My least favourite ingredient is a type of pepperoni a pizza chain puts on all their pizzas as standard. I've learned to ask for the New York style pepperoni and now I love their pizza. ☺

☐ **#9 Date**_____

Welcome to Watercooler Wednesday!

This week has just flown by. I really can't believe it's Wednesday again. How about you?

Last week, we talked about pizza, and there were some definite taste bud preferences. ☺

So to stay on the topic of food let's talk about ice cream!

What flavours of ice cream do you love? Which do you dislike? Have you invented any? Or found any flavours that are truly unique?

My go to flavour is chocolate chip mint, but anything with chocolate in it would probably do. ☺

And something tells me I'm going to be craving ice cream after I read everyone's comments. I may even be inspired to fire up our ice cream maker. ☺

And maybe the snow we're supposed to get today will start looking like ice cream. ☺ Have you ever had ice cream made from snow? I haven't, but I know some people love it.

☐ **#10 Date**_____

Welcome to another Watercooler Wednesday!

We've been talking a lot about food lately, and with yesterday being Pancake Tuesday, let's keep going! ☺

Did you eat pancakes yesterday?
What is your favourite type of pancake?

Do you like making them from scratch or from a mix? Or do you like eating them at a certain restaurant?

What toppings do you like or dislike?

Are you a maple syrup connoisseur?

We made pancakes from scratch yesterday. I've never made them from a mix. I love to put chocolate hazelnut spread on mine. But before I discovered that, I always put grape jam on top.

I still remember being the only one in my kindergarten class who ate jam instead of maple syrup. It's not that I don't like maple syrup, I just like jam on my pancakes better. ☺

And if you've never eaten pancakes, does this make you want to try them?

MARCH

☐ **#11 Date**_____

Welcome to Watercooler Wednesday!

Do you like to play chess?

How about checkers?

When you have the option to choose, do you like to be white or black in chess?

And in checkers, do you prefer to be red or black?

I've been playing chess since I was four, and the colour doesn't matter to me. I like being either. Same with checkers.

If you've never played, would you like to learn someday?

☐ **#12 Date**_____

Welcome to Watercooler Wednesday!

Do you have a favourite kitchen gadget?

I'd love to hear about a specialty item you have that makes your cooking or baking quicker or easier.

Or perhaps you have something in your kitchen that you just cannot live without.

Or maybe something decorative that brings a smile to your face.

Please share your favourites.

I think our cherry pitter is fun to use. And I love our green silicon spatula. But I don't think I could live without our jar opener. Not sure if Jason has ever used it, but I seem to pull it out enough for the both of us. ☺

☐ **#13 Date**_____

Welcome to Watercooler Wednesday!

Today is a special Watercooler Wednesday, because today it falls on the beginning of a new season!

So whether you're celebrating the advent of spring, or fall, today is a fresh beginning!

What are you looking forward to in the next few months?

Those in spring, do you participate it spring cleaning?

And if you're starting fall, are you ready to cozy up by the fire?

We're in spring here, and I cannot wait to see flowers pop up, birds return, green grass, leaves on the trees, and enjoy the fresh smell of spring air. ☺

☐ **#14 Date**_____

Welcome to Watercooler Wednesday!

Today is Pi Day. And yes, I spelled that correctly. It's Pi, as in the mathematical constant π which is approximately 3.14. But we're not going to do math today, instead we're going to talk about pie!

What is your favourite type of pie?

Do you bake pies?

Are there pies you only eat at certain times of the year?

Have you ever been in a pie eating contest?

Have you ever been a judge or entrant in a pie baking contest?

Have you ever seen a pie thrown in someone's face? Or had one thrown in your face?

I always associate pumpkin pie and apple pie with fall and thanksgiving, and cherry pie with Christmas. And I cannot name my favourite pie, but I do have some top favourites: pumpkin, apple, cherry, lemon meringue, chocolate, and banana coconut cream pie. Although I'm sure I'm missing some and can't wait for you to remind me, or introduce me to some new flavours. ☺

☐ **#15 Date**_____

Welcome to Watercooler Wednesday!

What is your oldest possession?

How old is it?

How did you acquire it?

I'm not sure if this is my oldest possession, but one Christmas I received a leather bound edition of Jane Austen's Pride and Prejudice from Jason. I've searched, and I think it may be from 1920. But regardless of its age, I love it! And the seller added in a page from a 1929 edition. I can only hope that the novel was in disrepair, because I can't imagine anyone with a love of books knowingly ripping one apart. And yes, I am one of those people who thinks it's an abomination to dog ear books. ☺

APRIL

☐ **#16 Date**_____

Welcome to Watercooler Wednesday! And the first Wednesday in April!

I grew up with the saying, "April showers bring May flowers."

Is it raining a lot this month where you live?

Do you like the rain?

I don't mind the rain. I actually like it when it's not freezing cold, and doesn't last for days on end. I need my sunshine. ☺ But on a hot summer day, the rain is sometimes welcome to help cool everything off and refresh the air. I also appreciate everything that grows because of it.

☐ **#17 Date**_____

YAY! It's Watercooler Wednesday!

Whether your beverage of choice is tea, coffee, or something else, today I thought we'd focus on our favourite mugs.

So let's see your mug shot!

And please, tell us why you love it?

I love mine because of its happy, positive message, and especially, its size: 26oz!

It's huge, but it's the only size that I have perfected my hot chocolate, mocha, and tea in. ☺

☐ **#18 Date**_____

Welcome to Watercooler Wednesday!

I thought today we'd discuss whether we're night owls or early birds.

There's a lot of research on the subject, but I thought we'd just have fun with the question.

Are you a night owl or an early bird (lark)?

Do you have the most energy in the morning and then your energy lowers as the day progresses, or do you start off with low energy and your energy rises as the day advances?

I'm a night owl. I always have been. My energy climbs as the day goes on.

☐ **#19 Date**_____

Welcome to Watercooler Wednesday!

Do you have a possession that holds significant importance to you?

Maybe something that was handed down to you or something that someone you love gave you?

Please share.

And if you can, we'd love to see a photo of it. ☺

I have so many items I treasure that it's hard to pick just one. For instance, all the gifts from loved ones that I've received over the years, I hold each one close to my heart.

I still have several pairs of booties/slippers my late grandmother knitted for me. She used to love to knit and was extremely prolific. It was fun to watch her hands move so fast, and she didn't even have to look at what she was doing.

☐ **#20 Date**_____

Welcome to Watercooler Wednesday!

Let's turn the clocks back…

What was the first book you remember reading or having read to you?

Did you enjoy it?

Did it change you in any way?

Although, this was definitely not the first book I read, the following is a very early memory of reading. I don't remember how old I was, but I remember my dad reading my brother and I, Peter Pan, before bed. We were always so excited, and of course begged for just one more chapter every single night. ☺

And I absolutely loved that my dad took us to the library every two weeks to bring back our borrowed books and pick out new ones. It was like getting new toys all the time!

MAY

☐ **#21 Date**_____

Welcome to Watercooler Wednesday on the First Day of May!

Today's question is an either or question.

If you could only drink one of these for the rest of your life, which would you choose, tea or coffee?

I apologize if this is an extremely difficult question, and takes some back and forth before you settle on your answer.

My tastes and preferences seem to change along with my eating habits, so every time I edit this book I write a different answer. I enjoy orange pekoe tea and lots of different herbal flavours. Plus, there's iced tea. However, I will choose coffee, because I think it would hurt me more if I was never able to drink it again.

Seriously, what an impossible question!

☐ **#22 Date**_____

Welcome to Watercooler Wednesday!

Mother's Day is celebrated on different dates throughout the world (if it is celebrated). But, here in Canada, Mother's Day is this weekend, so today let's talk about our Mothers or Mother figures, or if you prefer, special women in your life.

Do you have a fond memory of your mom, grandmother, etc. that you'd like to share?

What do you call your mom, grandmother, aunts, etc.?

Do you have any funny stories surrounding the worst or best Mother's Day gift(s) you've given or received?

Any traditions or things that you must do on Mother's Day?

Any special plans for this weekend?

My kids call me, Mommy. I call my mother and mother-in-law, Mom; the grandmother I knew and loved, Nonna or Nonnina; my aunts, Zia, Aunt, or Auntie. I adore these special women in my life and relish the opportunity to spoil them.

Happy Mother's Day!

☐ **#23 Date**_____

Welcome to Watercooler Wednesday!

Today's question is another tough one. ☺

As I write this, I'm not sure how I'm going to answer.

If you had to choose only one, for the rest of your life, which would you chose:

To watch movies or TV shows?

I'm going to choose TV shows. But I do hope that any movies I truly love will have TV spin offs. ☺

How about you?

☐ **#24 Date**_____

Welcome to Watercooler Wednesday! Today's question involves having us all pare down.

Hopefully we can find lots of different free things to do and open up our eyes to some new experiences.

What do you like to do that costs relatively little or no money?

I'll start off the list: I absolutely love walking/hiking.

Other things that cost virtually nothing: libraries (including all their programs), jogging, and visiting public parks.

Now it's your turn! Please share what you love to do that's free, or close to it.

And let's help each other plan some fun, cost effective activities!

☐ **#25 Date**_____

Welcome to the last Watercooler Wednesday of May!

Let's talk sports!

Do you have a sport you love to play?

Or maybe a sport you love to watch?

If not, perhaps a sport you played as a child?

Or tell us about something you think should be considered a sport. Like, for example, eating copious amounts of chocolate? I wholly support that bid.

I don't watch sports on TV, but I used to play a lot of sports as a kid, especially baseball, bowling, ping pong, basketball, and tennis. I also shot a lot of pool when I was a bit older.

JUNE

☐ **#26 Date**_____

Welcome to Watercooler Wednesday! It's June! We're halfway into the year!

I'm still not sure how that happened, but it seems like a good time to take stock of our goals and other things we wanted to accomplish this year. How are you progressing?

Are you on schedule? Close to your target?

Or have you just completely forgotten what you wanted to do this year?

I think I'm somewhere in the ballpark, but there's just so much I want to do this year, so I see a lot of work (ahem, it's not work if you love it, right?) in my future. ☺

☐ **#27 Date**_____

Welcome to Watercooler Wednesday!

This weekend, in Canada, we're celebrating Father's Day!

If you celebrate Father's Day, do you have any special plans or traditions?

Any funny or sentimental stories you'd like to share about your dad or a special father figure in your life? Or a story about the worst or best Father's Day gift(s) you've given or received?

Any traditions or things that you must do on Father's Day?

What do you call your dad, grandfather, uncles, etc.? I call my father and late father-in-law, Dad; the grandfather I knew and loved, Nonno or Nonnu; and my uncles, Uncle or Zio.

Happy Father's Day! Let the spoiling begin! ☺

☐ **#28 Date**_____

Welcome to Watercooler Wednesday!

In a couple days we're in for another season change! The start of summer for some, and winter for others!

Any big plans on the horizon? Anything you really want to do?

Something you're looking forward to?

Every year we make a family summer fun list where we write down all the things we'd like to do over the summer. This year we've already crossed off a few items and I'm so looking forward to doing the others! But just being outside is wonderful! I love the smell of water and fresh cut grass. Hearing and watching the birds. Seeing all the beautiful flowers, etc.

Do you rearrange your entire wardrobe when the seasons change so only the clothes and shoes you use will be out and the others are put out of sight? Or do you wear some of the same clothes all year round regardless of the seasons?

Or perhaps you don't need to rearrange anything because you live somewhere where the weather stays roughly the same all year? Please share.

☐ **#29 Date**_____

Welcome to Watercooler Wednesday!

Let's have some fun today!

Have you taken any great photos lately?

We'd love to see them!

Please share a photo of a landscape, person, pet, food, or anything else that's important to you.

And let's catch a glimpse into each other's worlds and hopefully learn something new!

I would have shared a photo of a dock we always find relaxing, where we usually see geese, turtles, fish, and ducks. But if we're really lucky we see beavers. ☺

☐ **#30 Date**_____

Welcome to Watercooler Wednesday!

Have you ever taken a trip in an RV (recreational vehicle)?

Where did you travel to in your RV?

Where did you park your RV overnight?

Did you enjoy this method of transportation?

What did you love about the RV?

Was there anything you disliked about the RV?

I've only been RVing once. We stayed at a campground. It was nice, and I liked it better than camping in a tent. It was comfortable and had all the amenities of home.

JULY

☐ **#31 Date**_____

Welcome to Watercooler Wednesday!

And the first week of July!

Let's talk about vacations!

Where is your favourite place to go on vacation?

Why do you love it there?

Who do you usually go on vacation with?

What type of accommodations do you enjoy?

For instance, do you like to stay at B&Bs, house rentals, hotels, motels, inns, or something else?

I like staying in hotels and love going on vacations to all different places. But rooms with views of water are always my favourite.

☐ **#32 Date**_____

Welcome to Watercooler Wednesday!

Hope your day is going great!

Here's today's question:

If you could make one local business where you live instantly become a successful international business, which one would you choose, and why?

I would choose a local bakery that has been baking my favourite Italian cakes, and other amazing desserts, for decades.

I wish I could send you all one of their cakes! Hence, why I'm choosing them. They're unbelievably delicious. And I'd love for everyone to experience them.

☐ **#33 Date**_____

Welcome to Watercooler Wednesday!

Since so many of us had great plans for this season, I thought we could talk about souvenirs!

Do you like to buy souvenirs or make them?

Any favourites?

Anything you collect? Or do you not like souvenirs?

On one of our more recent trips, we collected a ton of seashells. The kids used some to decorate pencil holders, and then we used some to make a photo frame where the shells on the frame are from the beach in the photo, so that's very special to us.

Anyone else have some neat do-it-yourself souvenir ideas?

☐ **#34 Date**_____

Welcome to Watercooler Wednesday!

Today's topic is going to get a little sticky because we'll be talking about jam, or do you call it jelly? Either way, let's get this topic started.

Do you have a favourite flavour?

Is there a flavour you don't like?

What do you love to put your jam or jelly on?

Is there something you won't eat unless it has jam or jelly on it?

My top two jam flavours are grape and strawberry. I've made strawberry jam, and nothing compares to fresh jam. The smell is amazing, and the taste is just so fresh and delicious. I like jam on pancakes, toast, and of course peanut butter and jam sandwiches. I also like cookies with jam filling, and doughnuts. But now I better stop, because this post is making me hungry. ☺

☐ **#35 Date**_____

Welcome to Watercooler Wednesday!

Today, I thought we could share apps that we like or find useful, so maybe we can all discover some great stuff!

Do you have any apps on your devices that you love?

Any apps that you think would help others?

Do you like to organize your apps? Or do you just leave them in whatever order you downloaded them?

I like to organize mine. I try to group them, and I always put the ones that I use the most on the first page.

Please share your favourite apps.

And here's a silly story. Once when Jason and I went out to dinner I was intrigued that the menu had a section titled "apps". As someone in Tech I wanted to check it out, because it would be cool to see what they had come up with, perhaps a game, a new way to order, or something else. Then I realized they meant appetizers. ☺

AUGUST

☐ **#36 Date**_____

Welcome to Watercooler Wednesday!

How is your summer/winter going?

Have you tried anything new this season?

Perhaps you tried a new food or drink?

Or maybe you played a new game, discovered a new place, or watched a new show?

Please share what's new in your life!

We recently tried riding a surrey bike, and it's tons of fun for the whole family to do together!

(Note: We've now biked in lots of different places, and it's still fun every time.)

☐ **#37 Date**_____

Welcome to Watercooler Wednesday!!!

Today's topic will be what we make it. ☺

Do you have any cool life hacks you'd like to share?

They don't have to be the best thing since sliced bread, just something that someone else may not have thought of and can use.

I've found that using clips on toothpaste tubes can help little hands, especially when they get near the end.

And putting a bowl of water in the oven when baking bread creates steam which improves the crust.

☐ **#38 Date**_____

Welcome to Watercooler Wednesday!

Today I thought we'd talk about the simple things in life.

For instance, if we were talking about food, would you agree that sometimes the simplest things taste so good?

For example, strawberries and whip cream, or toast and butter.

And if we were speaking about activities, maybe enjoying a walk, feeling a warm breeze, or listening to birds singing would top your list of favourite simple things?

Can you think of any simple things you love?

Please share!

And remember, photos are always great!

☐ **#39 Date**_____

Welcome to Watercooler Wednesday!

When you have to put something together do you like to read and follow the directions, or do you just jump in and try to figure it out on your own? Or perhaps you do some combination of the two?

Please share your process. And tell us what you built? And of course, whether you were successful or not?

For me, it depends on what I'm building. If it's complicated, I use the instructions. If the instructions are in another language that I can't read, which has happened, I'm forced to wing it. ☺

☐ **#40 Date**_____

Welcome to Watercooler Wednesday!

Has anyone had anything exciting or interesting happen to them lately?

Have you been out and about and discovered something you can share?

Maybe a photo of something neat, unusual, or something you learned?

I would share a photo about canoeing or pedal boating. There is just something so relaxing about being out on the water surrounded by nature.

SEPTEMBER

☐ **#41 Date**_____

Welcome to Watercooler Wednesday!

Where we live, it was the first day of school yesterday.

Do you have any memories of your first day back to school? Or maybe a memory you'd like to share from your school days?

Good Luck to everyone who is, or has loved ones, going back to school! Hope it's a great year!

I can remember my first day of grade two pretty clearly, because my friend and I thought we'd get ahead and copy everything off the blackboard before our teacher even asked. We worked hard and wrote as fast as we could until our hands ached. We were so happy after we'd accomplished it. But then we found out that the work wasn't for us! ☺

Eva Maria Hamilton

☐ **#42 Date**_____

Welcome to Watercooler Wednesday!

Normally, we don't talk about sad things here,
but today marks the Anniversary of 9/11. And
we couldn't let this day pass without
acknowledging it.

First, we'd like to offer our condolences to
anyone who may have been, or had loved ones,
affected by that tragedy. It was devastating,
and our hearts go out to you.

I can still remember that day quite clearly.
My day started with the sadness of knowing it
was a milestone anniversary for the loss of my
grandfather, and I'm still in shock over how
that day progressed.

Do you remember where you were and what you
were doing when you first found out about the
devastation?

Have you visited Ground Zero or the 9/11
Memorial or the 9/11 Memorial Museum in New
York City?

☐ **#43 Date**_____

Welcome to Watercooler Wednesday!

Can you believe there's less than a week left of summer/winter? That's right, the first day of fall/spring is coming up fast.

Are you looking forward to a new season?

Any interesting or exciting plans on the horizon?

Anything you're dying to do?

I'm sure we'll have a lot of leaves to rake, and like usual our collie, Daisy, will want to help. ☺

Do you notice your taste buds change at this time of year?

For instance, for those heading into fall, do you seem to want to eat more? Are you gravitating toward warmer food or comfort food?

And for those heading into spring, do you seem to want to eat colder food, or perhaps consume less food?

The squirrels are sure working hard here as fall approaches.

☐ **#44 Date**_____

Welcome to Watercooler Wednesday!

On your computer, phone, or other device, do you have a special photo set as your wallpaper?

Or do you just prefer to use whatever came with your device?

I thought it would be fun to see what everyone looks at every day.

On my laptop, I love to see a photo I took from Angel Island. Not only do I love the ferry ride from San Francisco, but there's beautiful scenery and wildlife to discover when you hike around the island. Aside from birds, we've seen deer, sea lions, and seals who sometimes lie on the docks. The island also has some interesting history and old buildings to explore. ☺

☐ **#45 Date**_____

Welcome to Watercooler Wednesday!

Since so many of us live quite a distance from each other, I thought it would be interesting to find out some of the local customs and/or traditions that exist where you live, or where you used to live, or even where you've visited.

For instance, in Southern Ontario, if the 13th of the month falls on a Friday, all the local bikers ride out to a town called Port Dover.

I can't wait to hear about the cool things where you live.

And even if you live close to someone, there may be something unknown to the other person you could unearth, so please share.

What are some of the local customs and/or traditions that exist where you live, where you used to live, or where you've visited?

OCTOBER

☐ **#46 Date**_____

Welcome to Watercooler Wednesday!

Do you prefer to rake leaves or shovel snow?

Or perhaps neither?

What is your favourite outside chore?

What is your least favourite outside chore?

I like raking leaves and shoveling snow. Both involve being outside, which I love.

Watering the garden, flowers, and the lawn are my summer favourites for sure. ☺ Although I do love to mow the lawn.

My least favourite chores would be anything to do with insects, like getting rid of spider webs or wasp nests.

☐ **#47 Date**_____

Welcome to Watercooler Wednesday!

Here in Canada, Monday is Thanksgiving.
To summarize: It's similar to American
Thanksgiving. For instance, most people eat
turkey with all the fixings. But it's more
about the harvest rather than Pilgrims. It's a
day where we bring to mind what we're thankful
for, and celebrate the harvest and autumn by
enjoying a big meal with family and friends.

Do you celebrate Thanksgiving or something
similar? What are you most thankful for?

I'm most thankful for my family and friends,
TestLauncher and our fantastic clients, every
awesome Launcher we get to work with, everyone
reading this, every good person striving to
make the world a better place, and every
blessing I have received.

There is so much to be thankful for every
single day and it's amazing how acknowledging
that gratitude keeps life full of positivity.

☐ **#48 Date**_____

Welcome to Watercooler Wednesday!

Let's talk about movies. But not just any movies—sequels!

Which sequels have you enjoyed?

Have you seen a sequel that was even better than the original movie? Which one? Why?

Are there any movie franchises where you wish they hadn't made a sequel to the original movie? Which ones? Why?

Are there any movie franchises where you hope they do make sequels to a movie you've seen? Which ones? Why?

Please share. I'm answering yes to all the above.

☐ **#49 Date**_____

Welcome to Watercooler Wednesday

Today's topic is mythical creatures.

If you could make any mythical creature real, which would you choose?

Alicorns (flying unicorns) popped into my mind first. They would give us a new way to travel, and they're magical.

☐ **#50 Date**_____

Welcome to Watercooler Wednesday!

Here in Canada, and in the United States, tonight is Devil's Night, and tomorrow is Halloween!

Do you celebrate Halloween?

Or perhaps, The Day of the Dead, All Saints Day, All Souls Day, or something else?

If you're giving out treats for Halloween, what goodies will the kids be lucky to receive?

Are you dressing up for Halloween? If so, as what?

I have yet to decide.

Do you like a scary Halloween or a happy Halloween?

I definitely like a happy Halloween.

But if you don't celebrate Halloween, here's a question for you: If you could be anyone or anything for a day, who or what would you be?

NOVEMBER

☐ **#51 Date**_____

Welcome to Watercooler Wednesday!

Can you believe there's less than two months left until the end of the year?

Looking back over the year, was there a newly released movie, book, or song that you really enjoyed?

Or perhaps there was something else that really made your year?

Please tell us about it.

Medical advancements always make me super happy. And of course welcoming a new puppy into our family.

Eva Maria Hamilton

☐ **#52 Date**_____

Welcome to Watercooler Wednesday!

Today, I hope we can inspire each other by helping one another.

What's the best piece of advice you've ever received?

One of the best pieces of advice that was drilled into me by my grandmother was not to worry. It can be much easier said than done, but she didn't just talk the talk, she truly did walk the walk. So I strive to follow her example, because as far as I've seen, she was 100% correct, things do have a way of working themselves out.

I also try to live by the advice from Benjamin Franklin, **"Don't put off until tomorrow what you can do today."**

And my dad also drilled into us, "There is no such thing as being bored, only boring people." And as I write this, I just overheard him telling our youngest daughter, "The impossible only takes longer."

☐ **#53 Date**_____

Welcome to Watercooler Wednesday!

Today's question might make us hungry, but hopefully it's an easy one.

How do you like your eggs cooked?

Maybe in cake? ☺

Or perhaps you don't like eggs?

I think if I had to rate my top three ways to eat eggs, aside from inside baked goods, they'd be: over medium, scrambled, and hard boiled. And as a drink, I love eggnog.

How about you? What are your favourites?

Any toppings or seasoning you must eat along with your eggs?

☐ **#54 Date**_____

Welcome to Watercooler Wednesday! Tomorrow is Thanksgiving in the States. Happy Thanksgiving to those celebrating! We've just recently talked about Thanksgiving, so I thought we'd talk about shopping in honour of Black Friday and Cyber Monday.

Black Friday has slowly crept into Canada, although our big shopping day, where people go looking for massive sales, has traditionally been Boxing Day, which is the day after Christmas.

Do you like shopping in stores, or would you rather shop online?

I can't imagine picking one over the other. I love being able to hunt down things online that would otherwise be next to impossible to find. But browsing in stores is also fun. Although, when I go shopping in stores, I do try to steer clear of crowds. Nevertheless, coming across something at a ridiculously low sale price never gets old.

☐ **#55 Date**_____

Welcome to Watercooler Wednesday!

Today's topic is tons of fun!

To participate, please post an obscure fragment of a photo.

Then, everyone can guess what everyone else's photos are.

Can you guess what mine is?

Next week, please tell everyone exactly what you posted, and hopefully show the entire photo.

Good luck guessing!

DECEMBER

☐ **#56 Date**_____

Welcome to Watercooler Wednesday!

Last week was so much fun!

I can't wait to see everyone's photos in their entirety this week!

I wonder if any of us guessed correctly?

My photo was of a tortoise that our eldest daughter got to feed. ☺

What was your photo?

Are there any other guessing games you can think of that we can play?

☐ **#57 Date**_____

Welcome to Watercooler Wednesday!

Before we get in to our topic, I just want to issue an ongoing invitation to send me any ideas you might have for Watercooler Wednesday, because your questions are always fun!

Now on to today's topic: Indoor Plants!

Do you like growing them? Did you have a lot growing up?

Do you have a lot now? Or perhaps you don't really care for them?

Are there plants you just can't keep alive or ones that grow out of control? Any favourites?

I like having indoor plants and can't remember ever not having any. My mom has always had lots. And it's always a sweet memory to remember my dad bringing her a poinsettia every Christmas. I like all different kinds of plants from cacti to palms. And for the first time ever one of our orchids rebloomed.

So what's growing in your home?

Or what do you wish was living with you?

☐ **#58 Date**_____

Welcome to Watercooler Wednesday!

Here's a fun holiday trivia quiz.

I'll post the answers next week.

Good Luck!

1. Who wrote, A Christmas Carol?

2. What real life department store is depicted in the movie, Miracle on 34th Street?

3. In the song, The Twelve Days of Christmas, how many gifts were given in total?

4. What are at least two other names for Santa Claus?

5. How many reindeer, including Rudolph, pull Santa's sleigh?

☐ **#59 Date**_____

Welcome to Watercooler Wednesday!

Hope you had fun playing trivia last week!

Here are the answers to the quiz:

1. Charles Dickens
2. Macy's
3. 364 (no wonder why it's such a long song ☺)
4. Kris Kringle, Saint Nick/Nicholas, Father Christmas
5. Nine

Now on to this week's question:

What is one activity you love to do over the holidays that really makes you feel like it is the holidays?

For me, it's playing games, and that includes anything from board games, to card games, to video games, or other types of games, like ping pong.

☐ **#60 Date**_____

Welcome to our last Watercooler Wednesday of the year!

Thanks to everyone who participates, and thus, makes Watercooler Wednesday so much fun, and something we all look forward to every week!

Go Team TestLauncher!

Wow! The new year will be here very soon!

Did you accomplish all your goals for the year?

What are your goals for the new year?

We're super happy about the direction TestLauncher is heading and we've got some exciting things in the works. So yes, we're definitely looking forward to ushering in a new year!

YEAR 2

JANUARY

☐ **#61 Date**_____

Welcome to our First Watercooler Wednesday of the year!

Hope everyone enjoyed a wonderful holiday season!

Does anyone have any holiday memories they'd like to share?

Did anything special or out of the ordinary happen?

Our eldest daughter saw robins flying over our backyard! They usually migrate south in the fall and come back in the spring, so I'm fascinated there are still some living here in winter. Does that mean we're going to have a warm winter or maybe an early spring?

☐ **#62 Date**_____

Welcome to Watercooler Wednesday!

Here's a hypothetical question:

If you were offered a round-trip ticket to space, would you go?

I wonder if this was a question they would have kicked around over a hundred years or so ago regarding flying in planes across the world?

At this point, I would say no.

But in the future, will these voyages be as normal and frequent as today's aviation trips?

☐ **#63 Date**_____

Welcome to Watercooler Wednesday!

Ready for some fun?

Share one photo you have on your phone, or
other device.

And please tell us about it!

I can't wait to see the world from your
perspective!

I originally shared a photo from a hike we
took, which clearly showed that a beaver must
have been nearby. ☺

☐ **#64 Date**_____

Welcome to Watercooler Wednesday!

I think today's question is next to impossible to answer.

Let's see if you agree with me.

What is your favourite type of cookie?

I think there are just too many delicious cookies to name only one.

I couldn't possibly choose between chocolate chip cookies, oatmeal raisin cookies, sandwich cookies, macaroons, shortbread, peanut butter cookies, our home-made honey cookies and Easter cookies, lady fingers, etc.

Hence my photo for this week is of some dog biscuits we baked. They're always a welcome treat. ☺

☐ **#65 Date**_____

Welcome to Watercooler Wednesday!

Here's the most simple question we have yet to

talk about:

What is your favourite colour?

I'd say mine is turquoise, or somewhere in the

green to blue spectrum. But pink and yellow

are also up there for me.

FEBRUARY

☐ **#66 Date**_____

Welcome to Watercooler Wednesday!

Have you discovered any new video games lately?

Or have you been involved in the same video game for a long time?

If so, what is it?

How are you enjoying your game(s)?

Anything you wish they would have programmed differently?

Answer to level up!

I haven't played an involved video game in a long time, but they are a lot of fun. There's nothing like that immersive experience where you get to explore and solve quests in order to progress through a game.

☐ **#67 Date**_____

Welcome to Watercooler Wednesday!

Do you prefer to read print books, ebooks, or listen to audio books?

I like all of them.

For instance, print books are great when I need to make notes, or I've been on the computer a lot and want some off-screen time. But ebooks are great when I want to bring books with me without the bulk, when I want a larger font to read with, or when there's low lighting. And Audio books are great for listening to when my hands aren't free, or when I want to read a book with other people.

How about you?

I'm sure we can come up with tons of positives, and maybe even some negatives, for every type of book.

☐ **#68 Date**_____

Welcome to Watercooler Wednesday!

Valentine's Day is coming up!

Whether you celebrate it or not, our oldest daughter came up with a great question for this week. Since Valentine's Day is about love, what do you love?

Because the question is what, not who, I'll put chocolate first.

But I also really love walking/hiking. And probably a whole host of other things.

But I'll only list a couple so I can jump in when someone else lists something I love. ☺

☐ **#69 Date**_____

Welcome to Watercooler Wednesday!

At the zoo, or in the circus, there are tons of exotic animals. But have you ever happened upon one of these creatures, by chance, in their natural habitat?

Was it an especially rare animal? Or perhaps a dangerous one?

How close did you get to it? And of course, what was it?

Once on vacation, I was walking along a path and had a tarantula cross right in front of me. It was only a couple of inches from my feet. Did I mention how much I don't like creepy crawly things? It was huge and hairy, and I'm still trying to erase that memory from my mind.

And when I was a teenager, I came pretty close to a creature, that at first looked like a large German Shepard, but on closer inspection, it was a cougar!

☐ **#70 Date**_____

Welcome to Watercooler Wednesday!

Today I thought it would be fun to think back
to some happy times when we were kids.

What is something you did as a kid that you
hardly ever, or never, do anymore?

I used to play a lot of baseball and bowling,
and I can't say I do that much anymore, not on
a team anyway.

Also, I can remember spending a ton of time at
recess and after school skipping when I was
really young.

MARCH

☐ **#71 Date**_____

Welcome to Watercooler Wednesday!

I hope we can have some fun today writing a story together.

I'll start with the first line and everyone can join in (multiple times if you wish) to add a word, sentence, or paragraph to move the story along.

I can't wait to see where this goes!

"Once upon a time, I was walking along a boardwalk with wetlands on both sides when I saw a hollowed-out tree in the distance…"

What happened next?

You decide.

☐ **#72 Date**_____

Welcome to Watercooler Wednesday!

I just discovered a new flavour of jam that I absolutely love—Cherry.

Wow!

It tastes just like the topping on cherry cheesecake!

Have you discovered any new tasty foods lately?

Or perhaps you ate something awful?

Please share your culinary adventures!

☐ **#73 Date**_____

Welcome to Watercooler Wednesday!

It's close to St. Patrick's Day, which always has great memes.

Have you seen any good ones?

If so, please share them.

And hopefully we'll all have the luck of the Irish with us.

Here's one by an unknown author:

May love and laughter light your days and warm your heart and home

May good and faithful friends be yours wherever you may roam

May peace and plenty bless you world with joy that long endure

May all life's passing seasons bring the best to you and yours

☐ **#74 Date**_____

Welcome to Watercooler Wednesday! The first day of spring/fall is here.

Usually we talk about our plans for the upcoming season, so why change that? ☺

What are you planning on doing this season? Anything you're looking forward to?

I always look forward to Easter. The chocolate, the beautiful pastel colours, the flowers, the promise of warmer weather to come, did I mention the chocolate? ☺

Do you get your home ready for the new season?

For instance, do you put certain items away or take others out and make sure they're clean and in working condition?

Do you have maintenance repairs and checks you perform for items in your home?

For instance, checking to see that your fire alarms work?

☐ **#75 Date**_____

Welcome to Watercooler Wednesday! Do you celebrate Easter?

Is hunting for Easter eggs part of your family's traditions? If it is, do you hunt for eggs inside or outside?

Do you dress up for Easter? Do you have Easter baskets? Have you ever taken part in an Easter parade?

What other traditions are part of your Easter celebration? And if you don't celebrate Easter, please tell us about some of your family's traditions.

Easter isn't just one day for our family. It starts on Thursday and lasts until Monday. Everyone enjoys indoor Easter egg hunts. Although, we have taken our kids to fantastic outdoor ones for charity. And then there's the food. Among other things, my mom always make special Easter cookies.

Happy Easter to those who celebrate!

APRIL

☐ **#76 Date**_____

Welcome to Watercooler Wednesday!

Have you ever had a crush on one of your teachers?

Just kidding! HAPPY APRIL FOOL'S DAY!

Please don't answer that question! ☺

Instead, let's talk about some of the good things that have happened to us recently.

The other day I had to cancel a couple of things and the people I spoke with were so nice it brought tears to my eyes. It was just lovely to deal with people who went out of their way to be kind.

So, please, share your stories so we can lift each other up by seeing the good in the world.

☐ **#77 Date**_____

Welcome to Watercooler Wednesday! Hope everyone is having a nice week!

Do you like to binge watch programs?

If you do, do you like to binge watch TV shows or movie franchises?

Or do you prefer to set a schedule so your viewing lasts longer?

I don't binge watch programs in terms of watching my screen for an entire day or weekend. Instead, I binge watch TV shows by finding ones that provide a lot of viewing hours, so that when I do get a chance to watch them, I don't have to waste time searching for something to watch. Plus, I know I have something good to look forward to for a long time.

☐ **#78 Date**_____

Welcome to Watercooler Wednesday!

Do you ever watch live cams?

There are so many! For instance, there are
ones that show different places around the
world, zoos, fish, litters of puppies, etc.

During the Covid-19 pandemic, our kids enjoyed
live cams about animals. There were a pair of
eagles raising their chicks and it was cool to
see them grow up and eventually fly away.

☐ **#79 Date**_____

Welcome to Watercooler Wednesday!

Today's question is super easy! The only possible problem is that it might make us hungry. ☺

Do you like potatoes? If so, how do you like them prepared? Mashed, baked, scalloped, in a salad, as French fries, chips, or some other way? There are so many ways to eat them!

I love mashed potatoes, and French fries smothered in gravy. But really it might be easier for me to think of how I don't like them. Although, as I write this I can't think of any. ☺ However, I've never eaten perogies, so I can't say for sure if I like them. But homemade gnocchi are amazing.

Ok, now it's your turn to make us hungry. ☺

☐ **#80 Date**_____

Welcome to Watercooler Wednesday!

Let's talk about cereal.

I don't know about you, but I'm always amazed at the sheer volume and variety that exist.

One of my favourites are Alpha-Bits. But unfortunately they were discontinued. I hope Post Consumer Brands brings them back one day.

Do you eat cereal?

Do you have any favourites?

Are there any that you absolutely won't eat?

Do you like to eat your cereal with milk or without milk?

If I'm eating cereal as a meal, I like it with milk. But if I'm eating cereal as a snack, then I like it without milk.

MAY

☐ **#81 Date**_____

Welcome to Watercooler Wednesday!

We've been talking about food lately, so I have another question:

What is your favourite meal of the day?

Is it breakfast, second breakfast, brunch, lunch, lupper/linner, tea, or supper/dinner?

Or do you prefer not to eat meals and just graze all day?

My favourite meal is definitely dinner. There are just so many options, and then there's dessert. ☺

☐ **#82 Date**_____

Welcome to Watercooler Wednesday!

On Sunday, it's Mother's Day here!

"Love as powerful as your mother's for you leaves its own mark."

-J.K. Rowling, Harry Potter and the Philosopher's Stone

Do you have any movies or books you love that celebrate motherhood?

I think the movie, Moms' Night Out, based on a book by Tricia Goyer, is fantastic!

☐ **#83 Date**_____

Welcome to Watercooler Wednesday!

Mother Nature decided to spice things up a little around here this past weekend by sending us a polar vortex, and thus, snow! In May! Today, however, it's supposed to be warmer.

What are some things you are loving about this season?

Lately, we've been passing by geese on our walks, and last week they came to show us their babies! It was so sweet. And there were so many of them.

Do you have things in your neighbourhood that you love?

For instance, do you have a splash park that's lots of fun, or a dog park that your dog loves? We do.

Or perhaps there are things in your town or city that you think are awesome?

For instance, does your city have a great sports team, or a fantastic beach?

Please share.

☐ **#84 Date**_____

Welcome to Watercooler Wednesday! Have you come across anything weird lately?

We've seen some odd things in our neighbourhood recently. For instance, a fire hydrant wearing a hat, a man standing on a hill looking at the sun like a scene out of the movie, City of Angels.

What weird sightings or stories can you share?

And I haven't issued a call for ideas for Watercooler Wednesday in a long time. But I always want them. So if there's anything we haven't discussed, or something you want to revisit, please message me. It always adds to our fun!

Now for your weird sightings or stories.

☐ **#85 Date**_____

Welcome to Watercooler Wednesday!

Hopefully everyone is enjoying a good week!

I thought we'd discuss what our favourite

indoor household chores are.

I'm going to pick a really fun and easy one

for this: watering the plants. ☺

What is your favourite indoor household chore?

Next week, we'll discuss our least favourite.

☺

JUNE

☐ **#86 Date**_____

Welcome to Watercooler Wednesday!

As promised, this week we'll be discussing our least favourite indoor household chores.

Mine is cleaning food particles out of the kitchen sink.

What chores make you groan, or worse, physically sick, when you're forced to do them?

Have you ever made a bargain or traded chores to avoid your despised task?

Or perhaps you pay someone to do it for you?

Please share.

☐ **#87 Date**_____

Welcome to Watercooler Wednesday!

Since we hang out around the Water Cooler
drinking water every Wednesday, I thought we
should talk about all the other drinks we
enjoy.

But first, what is your favourite way to drink
water?

I like club soda/carbonated water. Although
after I've worked out, just a glass of water
is good.

What is your favourite non-alcoholic beverage
besides water?

Mine is chocolate milk.

Do you consume different drinks during
different seasons?

I drink a lot more water and less warm
beverages in the summer.

☐ **#88 Date**_____

Welcome to Watercooler Wednesday!

This past weekend was Father's Day!

We hope those who celebrated had a fantastic day!

For Mother's Day we talked about moms in books and movies, so it only seems fitting to discuss dads now.

"Hey. Don't ever let somebody tell you...You can't do something. Not even me. All right?...You got a dream. You gotta protect it. People can't do something' themselves, they wanna tell you you can't do it. If you want something', go get it. Period."
-The Pursuit of Happyness

I can think of tons of movies that portray loving dads: Armageddon, Daddy Day Care, Father of the Bride, Mr. Mom, etc.

Can you name any movies or books that celebrate fatherhood?

☐ **#89 Date**_____

Welcome to Watercooler Wednesday!

Do you like to bake?

I do, but I like it a lot more when it's something I think is delicious. ☺ So I'm more partial to baking desserts. Although, bread is fun, too. And of course, more savoury dishes like pizza or lasagna.

What is your favourite thing to bake?

If you don't like to bake, what is your favourite baked good to eat?

And do you like to decorate baked goods?

I do. It's so much fun coming up with new and interesting ways to present cakes, cupcakes, pies, etc.

☐ **#90 Date**_____

Welcome to Watercooler Wednesday! And thanks to Jason for coming up with today's question!

Jason would like to see how many different uses we can come up with for an elastic band.

Hmmm...

I'll start:

1. To hold a box closed.
2. To attach things.
3. To make tie-dyed clothes.
4. For braces (on teeth).
5. To make a toy guitar.

Now it's your turn to keep the list going. ☺

What can you use an elastic band for?

JULY

☐ **#91 Date**_____

Welcome to Watercooler Wednesday!

Canadians celebrate July 1st as Canada Day!

In the United States they celebrate
Independence Day on July 4th!

With Launchers all over the world, which
holidays are unique to your country?

Please share them with us. ☺

Have you ever been in another country and got
to celebrate one of their holidays with them?

What happened? Did you enjoy it?

Are there any holidays that other countries
have that you wish your country had?

I may want to adopt a few after reading
today's answers.

☐ **#92 Date**_____

Welcome to Watercooler Wednesday!

Here's a question I don't think we've ever discussed before: Do you have a favourite umbrella?

Maybe you have one you love for rainy days, another for golfing, one for the beach, or some other type?

I've wanted a clear, bubble umbrella since I was a little girl, and last year in New York City I finally got one. ☺ Yay!

I also love self-opening and self-closing umbrellas.

Hopefully you can share a photo of your favourite umbrella.

☐ **#93 Date**_____

Welcome to Watercooler Wednesday!

As a child, my parents took us to amusement parks every summer.

Do you like going to amusement parks?

I used to go on all the rides, but now, I'm happy to watch or do other things.

Are there any rides you love, or perhaps hate?

Carousels are always fascinating because many of them hold such historical significance.

☐ **#94 Date**_____

Welcome to Watercooler Wednesday!

Jason thought it would be fun to ask if anyone is reading any books this summer/winter?

Are they fiction or non-fiction?

Are they Audio, ebook, or paperback books?

We'd love to know what you're reading. ☺

At the beginning of the year, I made my way through every Charles Dickens book I hadn't already read that my library had as an audiobook. ☺

☐ **#95 Date**_____

Welcome to Watercooler Wednesday!

It's the last Wednesday in July!

Let's end the month on a positive note.

What is the best thing that has happened to you this month?

We've been growing some vegetables and fruit, and this month we finally got a peak at some baby corn and watermelons.

Update: Squirrels ate all our corn and watermelons. ☺

AUGUST

☐ **#96 Date**_____

Welcome to Watercooler Wednesday!

Today's topic is silly, but hopefully fun. ☺

When you eat a sandwich, do you cut it or eat it whole?

If you cut it, do you cut it into halves lengthwise or diagonally? Or do you cut it into quarters? Or some other way?

The bread I use for sandwiches right now is kind of small and oval, so I don't cut mine. But when I was a kid and ate square bread, my sandwiches were always cut. I loved them cut into diagonal quarters. My next preference would be cut in half diagonally. But of course I still ate them however they were cut because they were always delicious! My mom made sure of that! She'd always make me what I loved: either chocolate hazelnut or grape sandwiches for my school lunches. ☺

And we'll leave the topic of whether you like your crust on or off for another day. ☺

After seeing some interesting ways to cut sandwiches online, I think I should start cutting mine the TestLauncher way, with a T and an L. ☺

I didn't have a photo of a sandwich so I used a photo of s'mores, because really aren't they a type of sandwich?

☐ **#97 Date**_____

Welcome to Watercooler Wednesday!

Let's pretend you were just woken up by your alarm.

Did you just hear beeping, music, or something else?

I would hear music. ☺

Do you get up when your alarm sounds, or do you shut it off and doze back to sleep?

I've always set my alarm early enough that I don't have to jump out of bed the moment it sounds.

☐ **#98 Date**_____

Welcome to Watercooler Wednesday!

We have a local country fair at the end of
summer every year that we've been
participating in for years. Our kids enter
their age level competitions for things like
art, crafts, photography, etc. We also love
seeing and petting all the animals. And of
course the atmosphere always exudes fun!
There's ice cream, need I say more? ☺

Do you go to any fairs or festivals?

What do you love about the fairs and festivals
you've been to?

☐ **#99 Date**_____

Welcome to Watercooler Wednesday!

Today's topic is for the birds. ☺

What is your favourite type of bird?

Perhaps you have a pet bird you love? Or had one as a child? Or you love seeing certain kinds of birds outside?

Do you love to feed birds? We love to feed 'our' ducks at a resort that feels like a home away from home to us.

Are there any birds that you love to hear sing?

Seagulls always remind me of summer, so I love hearing and seeing them because they instantly awaken such wonderful memories.

Please share your thoughts and stories about our feathered friends!

☐ **#100 Date**_____

Welcome to the last Watercooler Wednesday of August!

Is there anything you're looking forward to in September?

My parents both have birthdays in September, so I can't wait to celebrate them. ☺

Do you like to celebrate your birthday?

If you do, how do you like to celebrate it?

Do you have any birthday traditions?

Is there something you really want to do on your birthday?

My birthday is in the summer, so I like to party outside with the people I love.

SEPTEMBER

☐ **#101 Date**_____

Welcome to Watercooler Wednesday!

Here's something we haven't discussed yet:
Laundry.

Do you like to do laundry?

I do.

Are you a sorter or do you just throw
everything in all at once?

If you're a sorter, how do you sort your
laundry? By colour or some other method?

Do you like to dry your laundry outside in
warm weather?

In Portugal, it was neat to see everyone
hanging their laundry outside their windows or
on their balconies in the apartment buildings.

After your laundry is dry, do you fold it and
put it away immediately or does it hang around
in laundry baskets?

Or do you just get all your clothes dry
cleaned?

☐ **#102 Date**_____

Welcome to Watercooler Wednesday!

Do you own anything that you think someone

from another part of the world may not know

what it is or what it's used for?

Or maybe it's something from the past that you

think people may not know about anymore?

Please post a photo and let's have some fun

trying to figure out each other's items!

We can post our answers next week. ☺

☐ **#103 Date**_____

Welcome to Watercooler Wednesday!

Thanks to everyone who posted photos of interesting things last week. And thanks to everyone who tried to guess. It was lots of fun! ☺

Please tell us about what you posted last week. My photo was of a milk jug, because in Canada we can get our milk in bags, but then we need something to hold those bags. I suppose we could pour the milk into a container, but no one seems to do that. It's much quicker to drop it into a jug and then cut it open with a tool made specifically for cutting milk bags. Although, some people just use scissors.

Anyway, now on to today's topic: Outside Animals.

This year we've seen tons of skunks!

Do you have any interesting animals roaming around your area?

Eva Maria Hamilton

☐ **#104 Date**_____

Welcome to Watercooler Wednesday!

Do you have any flowers that grow wild where you live?

Aside from dandelions, we have lots, such as daisies, clover, Queen Anne's Lace, Cattails, etc.

I showed a photo of a Trillium that I took while hiking. It's the official flower of Ontario and grows wild on forest floors.

☐ **#105 Date**_____

Welcome to Watercooler Wednesday!

Today we're going to hit this topic out of the park, and talk about sports.

Do you have a favourite sports team that you cheer for? I don't. But I'd love to hear about yours.

Are you hoping your favourite team wins the Stanley Cup, Super Bowl, Grey Cup, World Series, NBA Finals, or something else?

I would love Super Bowl Sunday if it actually was a day where everyone ate a gigantic, 'super bowl' of ice cream with chocolate sauce, whip cream, and a cherry on top to really make it a 'sundae'. ☺

OCTOBER

☐ **#106 Date**_____

Welcome to Watercooler Wednesday!

Do you know of a place or an item that's been used in a TV show or a movie?

My parents' neighbourhood was being featured in a Canadian TV show and it was fun to see all the props and crew, and then later see them on the show.

Also, there's a historic village in Southern Ontario which has the train station used in the Canadian movie, Anne of Green Gables.

Have you ever seen things that you own used as props on TV shows or movies, such as cake plates, mugs, etc.?

We have, and that's always fun. ☺

☐ **#107 Date**_____

Welcome to Watercooler Wednesday!

Do you like to chew gum?

I've always chewed gum.

When I was younger, I chewed all the flavourful ones, and had lots of fun blowing bubbles.

Do you like to blow bubbles? As a kid, I was once in a contest at a festival to see who could blow the biggest bubble. I didn't win. I actually blew my worst bubble ever. ☺

Then, I progressed into more minty flavoured gum. Now, I chew mostly bubble-gum flavour. ☺

What is your favourite gum to chew? Have you always loved a certain flavour?

How long do you usually chew a piece of gum for? I get rid of mine pretty much as soon as they lose their flavour.

Did you ever get into trouble at school for chewing gum?

When is your favourite time of the day to chew gum?

☐ **#108 Date**_____

Welcome to Watercooler Wednesday!

Are you known for anything among your friends and/or relatives?

For instance, do your friends and/or family always ask you to bake something because they love one of your recipes?

Everyone who has ever tried my mom's lasagna always requests it. ☺

Or perhaps you're really good at making a craft, or playing an instrument?

Please tell us what your friends and/or family think you do really well.

Being in the tech field are we all asked to fix and/or set up people's devices? ☺

☐ **#109 Date**_____

Welcome to Watercooler Wednesday! And the

beginning of some *would you rather*

discussions.

Up first: Would you rather be able to fly or

breath under water?

I'd definitely pick flying. It would offer

such a different perspective seeing things

from above. Plus, it would be another great

way to travel. And if I ever came across a

tarantula or cougar again, I could just fly

away.

☐ **#110 Date**_____

Welcome to Watercooler Wednesday!

Here's another *would you rather* question:

Would you rather live in your favourite book or movie, or have the characters from your favourite book or movie live in your neighbourhood?

Since lots of my favourite books and movies are historical, I think I'd prefer to stay in this time period where we have modern medicine.

However, during the Covid-19 pandemic, a visit to another time and place would have been nice. ☺

NOVEMBER

☐ **#111 Date**_____

Welcome to Watercooler Wednesday!

Today's question is about something we all
seem to love:
Food. ☺

If you had to choose, would you rather eat
only warm food or eat only cold food?

That's a hard one, but I'd choose to eat all
cold food and give up all warm food, because I
think I may eat more cold food than warm food,
and a lot of the food that I usually eat warm
would also taste good cold.

How about you?

What would you choose?

Why?

And what foods would you then miss?

☐ **#112 Date**_____

Welcome to Watercooler Wednesday!

Today's question is a really hard one, so consider yourself warned. ☺

Would you rather eat the same food you love every day, but never be allowed to try anything new, or have to eat different food every day and never be allowed to eat the same food twice.

I'd eat the same food every day, because I can't imagine never eating the things I love ever again.

☐ **#113 Date**_____

Welcome to Watercooler Wednesday!

Today's question is another tough one.

If you could only ever eat one or the other, which would choose: To only eat fruit or to only eat vegetables?

I would choose fruit. But it would certainly be extremely hard to give up vegetables. Fortunately, tomatoes are botanically a fruit, so pasta and pizza would still be possible. ☺

And if you need help making your decision, other foods that most people consider vegetables but are actually fruit include: peppers, beans, peapods, avocados, squash, zucchini, cucumbers, olives, corn, pumpkins, and nuts.

☐ **#114 Date**_____

Welcome to Watercooler Wednesday!

If you were in charge of the weather, and got

to choose between making it rain or snow, what

would you allow to fall from the sky?

In the summer, warm rain is so nice, but when

it's colder out, I'd choose snow over rain.

☐ **#115 Date**_____

Welcome to Watercooler Wednesday!

What is one of your favourite older TV shows?

Perhaps there's a show you like from when TV shows were in black and white, such as Leave It To Beaver?

Or maybe you've never watched anything in black and white.

Please share.

Our dog, Daisy, who's a collie, gets called Lassie a lot, thanks to that black and white TV show. ☺

DECEMBER

☐ **#116 Date**_____

Welcome to Watercooler Wednesday!

Let's have fun talking about pasta!

What is your favourite type of pasta?

Do you like cheese or meat stuffed pasta?

Do you prefer tomato-based sauces, cheese-based sauces, or other types of sauce?

Or do you like your favourite pasta in a casserole or soup?

This is a really hard question to answer because there are so many varieties of pasta. So I'm going to have to just list some favourites. In tomato sauce, I like homemade gnocchi, spaghetti with ground beef, homemade fettuccine, meat ravioli, rigatoni and meatballs, homemade lasagna…It's too hard to stop, so I'll switch to alfredo sauce, which tastes so good with cheese ravioli.

Your turn.

Good luck choosing your favourite!

☐ **#117 Date**_____

Welcome to Watercooler Wednesday!

Here's a hint about what today's topic is:
Crazy Eights, Old Maid, War, Go Fish, Hearts,
Cribbage, Scopa, Uno, Euchre, Spoons…

Do you like playing card games?

Do you have a favourite card game?

I love playing cards. Rummy, Solitaire,
Euchre, and Poker are probably my favourites.
However, by Poker I mean Dealer's Choice not
just Texas Hold'em. I find Dealer's Choice
exponentially more fun because of the variety
and skill needed to play each type of game.
And there are tons! ☺

Do you play any card games that others may not
be familiar with?

Please share them.

☐ **#118 Date**_____

Welcome to Watercooler Wednesday!

If you could no longer live in the modern world and had to be sent back to a certain period of time in history, what time period would you travel to? And why?

Although people were pretty rough in biblical times, I think I'd go back to that time period. I mean if I'm already time travelling, hopefully I'd have some magical powers to keep me safe while I'm there. And give me the ability to see the things I want to see.

☐ **#119 Date**_____

Welcome to Watercooler Wednesday!

Do you have a favourite old movie?

I'm thinking of 'old' as in black and white, like Miracle on 34th Street, It's a Wonderful Life, Casablanca, Oliver Twist, Scrooge, and so on?

My mom loves the movie, The Bells of Saint Mary's, so I cannot even count how many times I've watched it.

But maybe you've never watched a black and white movie.

Are there any you'd like to add to your watch list?

If not, we can all answer what we like to snack on when we watch movies.

Popcorn, anyone? ☺

☐ **#120 Date**_____

Welcome to the last Watercooler Wednesday of the year!

I can't believe I just wrote that! Wow, the year went by fast!

But today's topic isn't about that, it's about gifts.

I love surprising people, and I always strive to give people gifts that make them super excited or speechless.

I remember one Christmas though when I was a kid, I received a doll that I instantly loved. I got to play with it on Christmas, but then it was recalled. Apparently, it was flammable and unsafe, and actually physically hurt some kids. Unbelievable, right? I was crushed. I did however get a replacement doll that I absolutely loved, so my story ends happily.

What was the best and/or worst gift you ever received? And what was the best and/or worst gift you ever gave someone?

YEAR 3

JANUARY

☐ **#121 Date**_____

Welcome to Watercooler Wednesday!

Did you make a New Year's resolution?

Or perhaps you chose a word or phrase that you're going to focus on to help guide you through the year?

Is there anything in particular you want to accomplish this year?

I always have a whole host of things I want to do. And it always seems to be more than humanly possible. But that never stops me from trying. And as Norman Vincent Peale said, "Shoot for the Moon. Even if you miss, you'll land among the starts."

☐ **#122 Date**_____

Welcome to Watercooler Wednesday! Let's talk about learning in our formative years.

What was your favourite subject in elementary school?

How about high school?

Any particular reason why you loved that subject?

Were there any subjects you didn't like? Why?

Again, it's probably easier for me to name a subject that I didn't like rather than name all the ones I really enjoyed. I seriously love learning and have taken a broad range of courses. In high school though, if I was pressed to say my least favourite subject, I think I'd have to say chemistry.

We've always homeschooled our daughters, and finding them hard at work learning always melts my heart.

☐ **#123 Date**_____

Welcome to a Watercooler Wednesday that's out there!

Do you think humans will ever get to other planets?

Why or why not?

I do. If you agree with me, how long do you think it will be before the first human makes it to another planet? Or lives on another planet?

Would you ever want to go to another planet?

If so, who would you want to go with?

☐ **#124 Date**_____

Welcome to Watercooler Wednesday!

Do you have a favourite piece of art that you love? Maybe from a favourite artist, or something you created, or someone you know made?

Why do you love that piece of art so much?

I used to have a picture of a guardian angel watching over two children in my room growing up, so that definitely holds special meaning to me.

☐ **#125 Date**_____

Welcome to Watercooler Wednesday!

What is your favourite musical instrument?
Why?

Do you play that instrument?

Or do you just love the sound of it?

Perhaps you just love the look of it?

Does it invoke a fond memory?

Like usual, I don't think I can choose just
one. I like how different instruments
emphasize each other. For instance, how an
entire orchestra can create such dramatic
music.

FEBRUARY

☐ **#126 Date**_____

Welcome to the First Watercooler Wednesday of

February!

If you could teleport yourself to any location

this weekend, where would you go?

Since it's so cold here, I'm thinking of

somewhere warm. ☺

☐ **#127 Date**_____

Welcome to Watercooler Wednesday!

If you were on the receiving end of a Valentine's Day gift, which of these three typical gifts would you prefer to receive:

- a stuffed animal

- a box of chocolates

- flowers

Or is there something else you'd prefer?

The perfect gift for me is always when it's heartfelt.

But if I had to choose from the three above, I'd choose chocolate.

☐ **#128 Date**_____

Welcome to Watercooler Wednesday!

What is your favourite video game of all time?

What device did you, or do you, play it on?

What is so great about it?

At the top of my list would be Maniac Mansion that we played on our Commodore 128. Trying to figure out how to progress through the game was challenging, but so much fun! And it was the first game I had ever played like that.

☐ **#129 Date**_____

Welcome to Watercooler Wednesday!

Depending on which pets you love best, be it anything from horses to rabbits, what is your favourite breed?

For instance, if you love cats, what cat breed do you like best: Siamese, British Shorthair, Abyssinian, or another type?

I love dogs! But I am partial to Collies and Shetland Sheepdogs. Although I could list so many more breeds I love.

As for birds, Cockatiels are super. Ours was so smart and friendly. He talked, cuddled, communicated with us, and always wanted to be with us.

☐ **#130 Date**_____

Welcome to Watercooler Wednesday!

What is your favourite way to exercise?

Do you exercise differently in the winter as opposed to the summer?

Do you like to exercise inside, outside, or both?

Do you like to exercise using machines or videos?

Do you enjoy exercising with other people or exercising alone?

Do you play music while you exercise? If so, what do you listen to? Or do you do something else, like watch TV while you exercise?

When is your favourite time of the day to exercise?

What does your pre-workout routine consist of? For example, do you have a list of stretches you do?

What does your post-workout routine consist of? For example, do you have a drink you must consume to rehydrate?

I like to do all sorts of things to challenge myself, and I love exercising outside and doing things that don't even feel like I'm exercising. But I also like exercising inside, and even watching shows while I exercise. Listening to music is always great, too.

MARCH

☐ **#131 Date**_____

Welcome to Watercooler Wednesday!

Today's question is an either-or question.

If you wanted to swim, would you rather go

swimming in a pool or at the beach?

I'm choosing a heated pool for swimming,

emphasis on the word heated.

But nothing beats walking along the beach. ☺

☐ **#132 Date**_____

Welcome to Watercooler Wednesday!

Today's question is hopefully an easy one:

What is your least favourite colour?

For me it all depends on how they're used and
where they are. Nevertheless, my list would
probably include brown (but never chocolate),
and red (but not at Christmas, Valentine's
Day, or Canada Day). ☺

How about you?

☐ **#133 Date**_____

Welcome to Watercooler Wednesday!

Are you going to wear green for St. Patrick's Day? I am. ☺

St. Patrick's Day is celebrated in Canada and the United States, and it's pretty much common practice that everyone is Irish on St. Patty's Day. So let's play a game to celebrate! Can you guess the meaning of the term, stall the ball?

It means to hold on or slow down.

Do you know of any other Irish sayings? Or are there any sayings in your culture which you think others may not understand?

I'll start. Do you know what a "kiki" is?

It's a party. So let's have a St. Patrick's Day kiki! ☺

☐ **#134 Date**_____

Welcome to Watercooler Wednesday!

Let's do something fun to kick off the start

of spring/fall!

Which animal do you think has the best, most

beautiful fur?

Please share a photo if you can.

I think rabbit fur is so soft. But then again,

so is alpaca wool. And some dogs feel like

cotton, too.

☐ **#135 Date**_____

Welcome to Watercooler Wednesday!

What is your favourite way to communicate, other than in person?

Do you enjoy talking on the phone?

Or do you prefer video chats?

Or perhaps you would rather talk through text?

Or send an email?

I would choose texting. It's quick. The other person gets the message immediately. You can respond when you're able. And if you're in public you can talk without having everyone hear your conversation.

APRIL

☐ **#136 Date**_____

Welcome to Watercooler Wednesday!

April Fool's Day is upon us!

Are you a practical joker?

Have you ever gotten anyone really good?

Good luck if you're planning a prank!

We'd love to hear about it, or about a practical joke you've witnessed.

Or perhaps you can just share a joke with us today. That would be fun!

And please don't ever cut brown 'E's out of construction paper and give them to me as brownies. I like chocolate way too much to appreciate that joke. ☺

☐ **#137 Date**_____

Welcome to Watercooler Wednesday!

Do you have a favourite pen colour?

I like writing in all different colours.

But what would you pick if you had to choose
between blue ink or black ink?

I would usually pick blue ink.

And yes, I definitely do have favourite pens.
But that is a topic for another time. ☺

☐ **#138 Date**_____

Welcome to Watercooler Wednesday!

If someone were serving you a drink, and asked you whether you'd like ice in your drink or no ice, which would you choose?

I usually opt for no ice, unless the drink is water.

For those who like ice, do you like real ice cubes, reusable ice cubes, or crushed ice?

Do you make your own ice in your freezer, in an ice maker, or do you like to buy it?

☐ **#139 Date**_____

Welcome to Watercooler Wednesday!

I know a lot of people enjoy discussing all things royal.

And if that's you, then this is your day!

Are you a royal watcher?

Do you have a favourite royal? It can be from any time period throughout history.

Do you have any favourite royal traditions, clothes, ceremonies, books, etc.?

If you were a royal, where would you live?

What would you like your title to be?

I'm not a royal watcher, so my favourites would have to include imaginary ones, like Belle from Beauty and the Beast, or Princess Twilight Sparkle from My Little Pony. Can you tell I have daughters? ☺

☐ **#140 Date**_____

Welcome to Watercooler Wednesday!

Can you believe over a quarter of the year has already passed?

We're well into spring/fall now!

Do you have a photo from the first quarter of the year you'd like to share?

Please do!

They're always so much fun!

My photos showed the before and after of a snow day that just happened out of the blue. Poor flowers, they must have been shocked. But that's spring. ☺

MAY

☐ **#141 Date**_____

Welcome to Watercooler Wednesday!

The start of May always goes hand in hand with May the 4th.

Do you like to say, May The Fourth Be With You, like Star Wars fans do, or May The Firth Be With You, as Jane Austen fans do?

I'm a Janeite. ☺

But we definitely can't forget to wish everyone a Happy May Day or Happy Cinco de Mayo!

If you're celebrating these holidays, please let us know how and share about them.

☐ **#142 Date**_____

Welcome to Watercooler Wednesday!

For a lot of us, it's getting close to growing season.

Do you have any plans, or are you still dreaming about what you'd love to plant this year?

If your growing season has already passed, or if you're in the thick of it, what things have you planted this year?

I love seeing and thinking about all the things there are to plant. I usually have to rein in my ideas though. Hence, I'm still in the planning process. But I'm thinking of growing even more vegetables and herbs this year. As for flowers, how to choose? Geraniums, marigolds, impatiens, petunias, begonias, roses…Seriously, aren't all flowers so pretty?

I wonder if we have different things we like to grow based on where we each live. So please, let's talk about what we're growing, or hoping to. And if you're not growing anything outside, please share what you're growing inside, or what you love to see other people grow.

☐ **#143 Date**_____

Welcome to Watercooler Wednesday!

Last week's post was awesome! I so enjoyed seeing and hearing about what everyone is growing, or planning to. I think we should make that into a regular monthly topic over the next several months so we can see everyone's progress. Or your neighbours, if you're not growing anything. ☺

Now onto this week's topic: Water Activities.

What do you like to do in or on the water? For example, do you like to go paddle boarding, swimming, scuba diving, rafting, boating, or some other activity?

I love being on the water. Cruises and pedal boating are two of my favourites.

If you don't like to go in or on the water, what do you do around the water instead?

☐ **#144 Date**_____

Welcome to Watercooler Wednesday!

What is your favourite flavour of cake?

I'll say chocolate in general, because there are just too many different types for me to narrow it down.

But then again, there are so many delicious cakes, like carrot cake, cheesecake, lemon cake, Italian cakes, etc.

Good luck answering this question.

It's sure to make us all hungry. ☺

☐ **#145 Date**_____

Welcome to Watercooler Wednesday!

It's getting close to the end of the month.

Did you learn anything new this month?

Please share anything you learned.

It can be something random and small, or something large and truly significant.

But if it wasn't this month, that's okay, anything recent will do.

In Canada, we have black, brown, and red ants. But this month, I learned that green ants exist! Apparently, they're endemic to Australia.

JUNE

☐ **#146 Date**_____

Welcome to Watercooler Wednesday!

And the first Wednesday in June!

Summer/Winter is on its way!

What are your favourite outdoor lawn games?

Do you enjoy badminton, horseshoes, lawn darts, frisbee, bocce, or something else?

I've always wanted to get one of those giant outdoor chess sets. It would offer such a fun, new perspective on playing chess.

But I would share a photo of our dog, Daisy. When she was a puppy she literally loved our tetherball to death. She would carry it with her everywhere and never wanted to part with it while she was outside. ☺

☐ **#147 Date**_____

Welcome to Watercooler Wednesday!

Do you celebrate your pets' birthdays? We do!

Our rough collie, Daisy, has the same birthday as Pal, the original Lassie, June 4th. And our smooth collie, Glory, is eleven years Daisy's junior. Amazingly, her birthday is four days before Daisy's on May 31st.

We love to spoil our puppies on their birthdays and try to do all their favourite activities and of course give them all their favourite treats.

How do you celebrate your pets' birthdays?

When are they?

☐ **#148 Date**_____

Welcome to Watercooler Wednesday!

In honour of Father's Day (and Mother's Day last month) do you think we can make a list of all the things that have the word mother or father in it, or their synonyms, such as mom or dad?

I'll start:

- Father Time

- Mother Nature

- Mother Earth

- Mom and Pop Shop

- Pop (as in soda pop)

☐ **#149 Date**_____

Welcome to Watercooler Wednesday! Let's have some fun with Wi-Fi names.

Have you seen any Wi-Fi names that were really weird?

How about some Wi-Fi names that you think are awesome?

Are there any Wi-Fi names you think would be cool?

For example, HauntedLighthouse.

Are there any Wi-Fi names you think would scare your neighbours?

For example, Stakeout1005. ☺

☐ **#150 Date**_____

Welcome to Watercooler Wednesday!

It's been over a month since we first talked about what we're growing.

How has everyone progressed?

Photos are always great, but telling everyone is good, too!

However, if you're not growing anything, perhaps you love something in your neighbourhood or you have an idea about something you wish you were growing.

I cannot wait to taste our peppers and tomatoes. But since they aren't quite ready, I just love to smell them. ☺ It's one of the reasons I love to grow mint.

Do you ever take notice of where in the world the produce you buy comes from? I do.

What is one thing that is grown in another country that you wish you could grow?

I'd love to be able to grow citrus fruit.

JULY

☐ **#151 Date**_____

Welcome to Watercooler Wednesday!

For the next several weeks, I have some silly, but interesting, questions to think about and debate.

Here's the first one:

Is cereal soup? Why or why not?

I vote yes. There are types of cold soup. And cereal does have grains floating in a liquid. ☺

If you have any other silly, but interesting, questions please message me, and we'll discuss them in the coming weeks.

Eva Maria Hamilton

☐ **#152 Date**_____

Welcome to Watercooler Wednesday!

Here are this week's silly, but interesting, questions for us to discuss:

Is a hotdog a sandwich? Why or why not?

I'm on team yes it's a sandwich, because the meat, and anything else a person adds on top of it, sit between two pieces of bread.

And here's a tougher question: Do you think corndogs are sandwiches? Why or why not?

I suppose since the meat is surrounded by bread I'll vote that yes it is a sandwich.

What do you think?

☐ **#153 Date**_____

Welcome to Watercooler Wednesday!

We've been asking some silly questions lately, which have produced some really interesting and yummy answers, so here's another one:

Do you consider tomatoes to be a fruit or a vegetable? Why or why not?

I know they're technically fruit, but I think of them as vegetables. Unlike fruit, I never bite into a tomato and eat it whole like I would with say an apple, although I know some people do. But it's also not sweet, and I usually think of fruit as sweet. How about you?

☐ **#154 Date**_____

Welcome to Watercooler Wednesday!

Here's yet another silly, but interesting, question for discussion:

Is pizza pie? Why or why not?

I know there are meat pies and chicken pot pies, but when I think of pie I usually think of them as desserts, or having fruit in them like cherry pie. I also tend to think of pie as having more depth than even deep-dish pizzas. So my vote is no, they're not pie.

But my taste buds really don't care what my brain has to say on the subject as long as pizza is being served and there's pie for dessert. ☺

☐ **#155 Date**_____

Welcome to the last Watercooler Wednesday of July!

Let's see and hear about how everyone's plants are growing.

Are your plants thriving or barely holding on?

Have you harvested anything?

I thought we were going to lose our tomato plants, but they're hanging in there. So far we've had a handful of cherry tomatoes, a cucumber, and a few beans.

If you haven't harvested anything in your own garden, have you ever gone to a farm to pick your own produce?

What did you pick?

Did you have fun?

I have such great memories picking strawberries and tomatoes.

AUGUST

☐ **#156 Date**_____

Welcome to Watercooler Wednesday!

For a lot of us, it's the middle of summer.

Do you have anything that you must do in summer?

Something that you have to do or it's just not summer?

For me, going to a local conservation area is a definite must during summer. Growing up we used to go almost every weekend, and our day trips were always so much fun. I cannot ever imagine not getting to revisit some of our favourite spots and be flooded with memories from our family's special times there. Plus, I love being immersed in nature.

☐ **#157 Date**_____

Welcome to Watercooler Wednesday!

Have you ever gone fishing? Did you enjoy it?
If not, why?

If you do like fishing, where do you like to
go fishing?

What kinds of fish do you like to catch?

Do you eat what you catch or do you release
them?

As a kid we used to fish off a bridge at our
favourite conservation area. It was lots of
fun! We used worms as bait, but never really
caught much, usually just catfish. And we
always released them after.

☐ **#158 Date**_____

Welcome to Watercooler Wednesday!

Today's question is for chocolate lovers.

Think about the best chocolate cake you've ever eaten.

Now think about the best chocolate brownie you've ever had.

Which one was better, the chocolate cake or a chocolate brownie?

This is so tough. Seriously, it's really difficult! I suppose I'll choose the brownie though, because that will just mean that I need to keep sampling chocolate cakes to make sure I did indeed make the right choice. ☺

☐ **#159 Date**_____

Welcome to Watercooler Wednesday!

What is your favourite way to cool off in the summer?

Do you like to:

- have a cold drink

- eat ice cream

- run through a sprinkler

- sit in front of a fan

- stick your head in the fridge

- jump in a pool

- or something else?

Please share.

I think it's always fun to use the mist sprayer on the garden hose to cool off. ☺

☐ **#160 Date**_____

Welcome to the last Watercooler Wednesday of August!

Being the last one, we'll stick with what we've been discussing all season: Plants.

Our oldest daughter has been trying to grow a pumpkin since spring. Her pumpkin plant has leaves that remind me of elephant ears because they're so big! However, every time it gets a flower (and there have been several) it somehow gets knocked off and so she has yet to produce a pumpkin. But we've now fortified her pumpkin, and fingers crossed, she'll get to grow a good-sized pumpkin for Halloween.

Update: She did! And she continues to love growing pumpkins.

How are your plants doing?

Are your flowers still in full bloom, or do they look like they're ready for fall to take over?

Do you plant or grow popular fall plants like chrysanthemums?

SEPTEMBER

☐ **#161 Date**_____

Welcome to Watercooler Wednesday! And welcome to September! Today we're talking about cheesecake.

Do you like cheesecake? If not, do you like any other desserts with cheese in them, like Tiramisu?

There are so many different flavours of cheesecake, and people keep inventing new ones!

If you perform a search you'll see what I mean, and you may come to the same conclusion as me: I have seriously neglected my cheesecake tasting. ☺

What is your favourite kind of cheesecake?

And if it's too hard to narrow it down to just one, maybe you can list some of your top picks?

☐ **#162 Date**_____

Welcome to Watercooler Wednesday!

This week will be for the coffee drinkers.

And next week, for the tea lovers.

So let's discuss, anything and everything to do with, coffee.

Describe your favourite cup of coffee?

I like mochas (coffee mixed with cocoa and milk).

Do you like anything else related to coffee, such as chocolate covered espresso beans, coffee cake, or something else? I answer yes to all of these and add tiramisu.

Have you ever been to a coffee plantation? We have. It was lovely, and we learned so much.

Do you have a favourite coffee machine or café where you purchase your coffee?

☐ **#163 Date**_____

Welcome to Watercooler Wednesday! Last week we had a great discussion about coffee. This week it's all about tea.

Do you prefer tea bags or loose-leaf tea?

Do you have a favourite flavour?

Do you adhere to a certain procedure in making your tea?

Is there anything you usually eat with your tea?

When is your favourite time of day to drink tea?

I'd love to hear about whatever makes your tea experience wonderful!

For convenience, I use tea bags. And I mostly enjoy orange pekoe or herbal tea. But sweetened iced tea is good, too.

I have never been to a formal tea in a proper tearoom, have you?

☐ **#164 Date**_____

Welcome to Watercooler Wednesday!

Today is the first day of autumn/ spring!

What are you looking forward to this season?

I'm looking forward to all the holidays, with all the fun they bring. ☺

Do you have any traditions to kick off this new season?

I only buy apple cider in the fall, and I just bought some to kick off our new season. I cannot wait to heat it up, because the house is going to smell so good. ☺

If it were spring here, I like to kick off spring by buying flowering bulb plants, like hyacinths, and then planting them outside when it's warm enough. I love the first flowers of spring and the anticipation of seeing them burst to life every year.

☐ **#165 Date**_____

Welcome to Watercooler Wednesday!

Besides medical advancements, what is one invention that you couldn't live without?

I think one of the all-time greatest inventions is indoor plumbing. Perhaps for those who live in warmer climates this may not rank as high, but just imagine getting water from a well in -20°C/-4°F, or having to use an outhouse in the middle of the night in a blizzard.

We really do have so much to be thankful for!

Also, if you have any ideas for future Welcome To Watercooler Wednesdays please send me your questions. ☺

OCTOBER

☐ **#166 Date**_____

Welcome to Watercooler Wednesday!

I think today's question is a hard one.

If you were a bird, would you rather be a pet and have a nice, safe home with a constant supply of food and water, or would you rather be a wild bird, free to go wherever you want but with all the dangers and uncertainty that comes with that, like predators, inclement weather, and food shortages.

I think I'd rather be a pet, because I'd hate to live constantly watching my back for predators. Hopefully, my owners would bring my cage outside in warm weather though, and of course let me fly around the house. Also, most animals live longer in captivity than in the wild.

So what would you choose?

And why?

☐ **#167 Date**_____

Welcome to Watercooler Wednesday!

In honour of Canadian Thanksgiving this weekend, let's have a virtual celebration dinner.

I've brought the turkey.

What food, drinks, or decorations do you usually have at Thanksgiving, or other celebrations, that you would like to bring to our feast?

Bon Appetite!

Or should I say, Gobble Gobble. ☺

☐ **#168 Date**_____

Welcome to Watercooler Wednesday!

Have you discovered any new music you like to listen to?

Or perhaps you're happy listening to a group or artist you've always loved.

Please share your favourites.

I listen to all sorts of music. But I never tire of Oldies. Too many great memories. ☺

☐ **#169 Date**_____

Welcome to Watercooler Wednesday!

Have you seen any good movies lately?

Or maybe you've watched a good documentary, or a TV show you thought was great?

Please share any recommendations you have.

I watched a choose-your-own-adventure movie with our girls. It was really neat to get to make decisions that affected the outcome of the movie. And it was very interesting to see what each of our daughters picked versus what I would choose.

☐ **#170 Date**_____

Welcome to Watercooler Wednesday!

Halloween is coming up!

Are you dressing up for Halloween?

If so, what will you be dressing up as?

If you don't celebrate Halloween, but were to

dress up, what would you want to dress up as?

This year, I think I'll be a jack-o'-lantern.

If you have any spooky photos, please share

them.

NOVEMBER

☐ **#171 Date**_____

Welcome to Watercooler Wednesday!

We're travelling back in time today.

Is there anything you didn't like as a kid
that you like now?

It could be a type of food, or a game, or
music, or anything really.

I'll start:

I never ate fish when I was younger, but as an
adult, I like some types of fish.

☐ **#172 Date**_____

Welcome to Watercooler Wednesday!

We're travelling back in time again to play with the question from last week in a different way.

Is there anything you liked as a kid that you don't like now?

Again, it could be a type of food, a game, music, etc. Perhaps you used to love playing in the snow, but not now?

I'll start: I used to like to ride roller coasters, but not now.

Welcome to Watercooler Wednesday!

Hope you're ready for more time travelling.

Is there anything you didn't like as a kid that you still don't like?

I'm thinking there might be a lot of people who would say Brussel sprouts.

I'm going to say bugs though. I've never liked bugs and I still don't.

And as always, if you have any questions for Welcome To Watercooler Wednesday, please message me your ideas. Thanks!

☐ **#174 Date**_____

Welcome to Watercooler Wednesday!

And the time travelling continues.

Is there anything you liked as a kid that you still like now?

This would be an endless list for me, so I'll just name a few: dogs, Christmas, and chocolate.

☐ **#175 Date**_____

Welcome to Watercooler Wednesday!

Tomorrow is American Thanksgiving! And that is always followed by Black Friday and Cyber Monday.

Are you in the market for something specific?

Perhaps another Launcher can help you find a good deal.

Pre-Black Friday deals are already in full swing.

So for this week's Welcome To Watercooler Wednesday, please share links to any really good shopping deals you find.

Happy Thanksgiving and Happy Shopping!

DECEMBER

☐ **#176 Date**_____

Welcome to Watercooler Wednesday!

Can you believe it's the first day of December?

What are you looking forward to this month? Any special plans?

What are some traditions you participate in this month?

What do you love, and/or dislike, about December?

Do you find December to be a really tiring month because perhaps you have a lot to do, or do you find it invigorating?

I don't like that it gets dark so early. However, I'm looking forward to our Holiday Party, and of course the holidays and everything that goes along with them. I'm definitely a fan of December! ☺

☐ **#177 Date**_____

Welcome to Watercooler Wednesday!

There's only a little over three weeks left in this year.

What are you looking forward to in the coming year?

I'm looking forward to some new adventures, and more of all the great things in our lives.

At this time next year, what do you hope your life will look like?

For example, are you hoping to get a new pet next year? Or maybe change your hairstyle? Or move?

And if you don't want to predict what your life will look like in a year from now, what do you think will be different in our world next year?

World peace is always something to hope for.

☐ **#178 Date**_____

Welcome to Watercooler Wednesday!

The fast-approaching holidays have me thinking of the past. So let's talk about the video games we played as children.

What video game was your favourite?

Did you think some video games were too easy?

Do you remember any video games you didn't like, or any that you thought were really hard back then? Do you still find them hard now?

Are there any you haven't played in years, but would love to play again? I'd love to have a crack at them all again! ☺

We had a tabletop video game, and as a family we'd have tournaments. It was lots of fun and I have wonderful memories of that time spent together.

☐ **#179 Date**_____

Welcome to Watercooler Wednesday!

As a kid, what did you look forward to the most at this time of year?

I looked forward to spending time with my family and friends. We always had lots of parties at our house. On Christmas Eve we would go over to my Grandparents' house. Then on Christmas Day we'd have a big party at our house. And on New Year's Eve we'd have another big party at our house. And in between Christmas and New Year's Eve it would be just day after day of fun and games. Add in the great food, and seriously what's not to love? ☺

☐ **#180 Date**_____

Welcome to the last Watercooler Wednesday of the year!

What a year it's been!

Let's take a look back.

What is one of your favourite or most memorable moments at TestLauncher?

Did you find a bug that stands out in your mind?

Did you receive a wonderful compliment from a TestLauncher client?

Did you have a great experience working with a teammate?

Let's reminisce and share some positivity!

Jason and I are thankful for everyone on Team TestLauncher! And it always means so much to us when you tell us how much you enjoy working at TestLauncher! Thank you!

Let's keep making TestLauncher great!

Happy Holidays!

We wish you every happiness in the new year!

YEAR 4

JANUARY

☐ **#181 Date**_____

Welcome to the first Watercooler Wednesday of the New Year!

We hope everyone enjoyed a really nice holiday season!

We'd love to hear about it! Did anything crazy or funny happen?

We have a fresh new year ahead of us with so much to look forward to! What are your hopes for this year?

Is there anything you're not looking forward to?

I'm going to keep looking for the good in everything.

As always, if anyone has any topics they'd like to discuss this year just message me your ideas any time throughout the year.

And welcome back!

Let's make this year awesome!

☐ **#182 Date**_____

Welcome to the second Watercooler Wednesday of the New Year!

The holidays are already starting to seem like a long time ago. But they were actually only a couple of weeks ago.

If you could invite someone alive, someone from history, or a made-up character to your house for the holidays, who would you invite?

Alternatively, if you could take everyone you usually spend the holidays with to someone's home, be it someone alive, someone from history, or a made-up character's home, where would you spend the holidays?

So many options. So many possibilities. How to decide?

Inviting someone magical over would be fun, especially if they enjoy using their magic for good. ☺

☐ **#183 Date**_____

Welcome to Watercooler Wednesday!

We just had the first snowstorm of the year in Southern Ontario. But I won't say too much about it so others can jump in with their experiences.

Our dog, Daisy, absolutely loves the snow! She loves to play in it, lie in it, and of course eat it. ☺ Do your pets love the snow?

Do you love snow?

If you do like snow, what activities do you like to do in the snow? For example, do you like to make snow people, have snowball fights, ski, snowboard, snowshoe, go dogsledding, or some other activity?

Or perhaps you just like the way it looks and prefer to stay indoors where it's warm?

If you live where it doesn't snow and have never seen snow, would you like to experience it?

☐ **#184 Date**_____

Welcome to Watercooler Wednesday!

Here's a fun question: What is your favourite animal that is native to where you live?

We have so many wonderful and cute animals around here that it's really hard to choose. But one animal that always stands out is a tiny bird called a Golden-Crowned Kinglet. They are so cute and they're not afraid of people. If you come across one it will actually go on your hand, without food, just like a pet.

Another really cool animal around here, that you can consider yourself lucky if you ever to get to see, is a beaver.

And it's always exciting to find a bird's nest, like the robin's nests we have the honour of enjoying every year as we watch the sweet babies grow and eventually fly away.

And there are so many more I could list! But I won't, because I can't wait to see what you share! ☺

☐ **#185 Date**_____

Welcome To Watercooler Wednesday! Say Cheese!

Have you grown up being told to 'say cheese' whenever someone takes your picture? Or do you say something else? Perhaps you simply just smile, or pose a certain way?

Whatever you do, please share a photo of yourself or whatever you've just taken a photo of. And of course, please tell us about it.

I took a photo of a hiking trail to show everyone that for a good part of the trail people made two paths, but then all of a sudden, the two paths vanished and there was only one, which really begged the question of what happened to the people who had forged that second path? Did they just magically disappear? Because later the two paths resurfaced, so the people must have reappeared. But only to disappear again! Sure, they could have gotten tired of trampling through the snow and walked single file behind each other, which is easier. But I prefer to think that we walk in a magical wood. ☺

FEBRUARY

☐ **#186 Date**_____

Welcome to Watercooler Wednesday!

Happy Groundhog's Day!

Canada and the United States will soon find
out if there will be six more weeks of winter
or an early spring, thanks to groundhogs,
like: Wiarton Willie, Manitoba Merv,
Shubenacadie Sam, Winnipeg Wyn, Balzac Billy,
Fred la Marmotte, Okanagan Okie, Punxsutawney
Phil, and many others.

What are you hoping for?

Please chime in even if your country doesn't
follow this tradition.

And if you're in the Southern Hemisphere, are
you hoping for more hot summer weather or are
you ready for the cooler days of fall?

☐ **#187 Date**_____

Welcome to Watercooler Wednesday!

Are you a fan of the Olympics?

Do you prefer the Summer or Winter Olympics?

Are there any sports you love to watch?

Do you play any of the sports?

Are there any athletes you really cheer for?

Any countries, besides your own, that you root for?

Have you ever attended the Olympics?

Please share.

I like to watch the opening and closing ceremonies, but I don't usually watch much else.

☐ **#188 Date**_____

Welcome to Watercooler Wednesday!

In honour of Valentine's Day, what is your favourite romance movie?

Or if romance movies aren't your thing, perhaps there's a movie you like that has a romantic subplot in it, like Lord of the Rings?

And if that's still too much, what movie do you like to watch at this time of year?

One of my favourites is the 1995 BBC version of Jane Austen's Pride and Prejudice. It's so funny, and Mrs. Bennet is hilarious.

☐ **#189 Date**_____

Welcome to Watercooler Wednesday!

What is your all-time favourite car or

vehicle?

I don't really have one, so I'm going to

choose an ice cream truck. The sound of their

music playing always garners a smile. ☺

☐ **#190 Date**_____

Welcome to Watercooler Wednesday!

Here's a question some people may find hard:
If you could only put one topping on your
pizza, besides sauce and cheese, what would
that one topping be?

I'd choose pepperoni.

But just in case that question ended up being
too easy, here's another one: Do you have a
preference for how your pizza is cooked? For
instance, are you fine with cooking it in the
microwave, or do you prefer it cooked in a
commercial pizza oven, a wood pizza oven, or
something else?

I try to avoid cooking anything in a
microwave.

And now onto the eating part: How do you like
to eat your pizza, with your hands or with a
knife and fork?

I like both, it depends on the situation and
the pizza. ☺

MARCH

☐ **#191 Date**_____

Welcome to Watercooler Wednesday!

Do you like to create art? For instance, do you like to colour, draw, paint, sculpt, take photos, or create with other mediums?

Or is art something you only did as a kid?

Or perhaps you simply just like to appreciate great art?

Have you ever been to an art gallery? Did you enjoy it? Did you see anything you loved, or something unusual or interesting?

And if you've never been to an art gallery, is there one you'd like to visit?

I love creating art, and we have a local art gallery that hosts wonderful programs for children and families. .

☐ **#192 Date**_____

Welcome to Watercooler Wednesday!

Have you ever heard of the expression, "Beware the Ides of March?"

Do you believe that March 15th is a bad day?

There's plenty of other folklore that warns about bad fortune. Can you think of any? Do you believe any of them?

I'll start off the list:

- Opening an umbrella in the house
- When a black cat crosses your path
- Friday the 13th
- Breaking a mirror

Please add some folklore you've heard of.

☐ **#193 Date**_____

Welcome to Watercooler Wednesday!

Do you celebrate St. Patrick's Day?

Hopefully you'll celebrate with us today, and share some Irish sayings to uplift everyone, like these ones from unknown authors:

"May your troubles be less,

Your blessings be more,

And nothing but happiness

Come through your door"

"Always remember to forget

The things that made you sad,

But never forget to remember

The things that made you glad"

☐ #194 Date_____

Welcome to Watercooler Wednesday!

Hope your spring/fall is off to a good start!
Have you noticed any signs of the changing
season where you live? Here it's spring, and
one of the biggest things that I love is the
return of so many birds.

But now onto today's topic, which is hopefully
something we all like: Fountains.

Do you have any water fountains you love?

Does your city or town have any?

What do you love about these fountains?

Or perhaps you've seen some wonderful water
fountains on vacation?

Do you find water fountains relaxing?

Do you like to throw a coin into the water and
make a wish? Have they ever come true?

I absolutely love water fountains of all
shapes and sizes! I find them so mesmerizing
and beautiful!

☐ **#195 Date**_____

Welcome to Watercooler Wednesday!

Let's play a game today using anagrams.

Can you think of a word or phrase and then use those same letters to spell a different word or phrase?

I'll start:`

March = Charm

Eleven Plus Two = Twelve Plus One

Mommy = My Mom

Your turn. ☺

I wonder how many we can come up with.

Some of them are pretty neat!

APRIL

☐ **#196 Date**_____

Welcome to the first Watercooler Wednesday of April!

Last week we played with words, so this week let's play with numbers.

Using only addition, can you make a sum of 1000 with only eight 8s?

I'll post the answer next week. ☺

Good luck!

P.S. I haven't mentioned this in a while, but as always, if you have any questions you'd like to ask on Welcome To Watercooler Wednesday please message me.

☐ **#197 Date**_____

Welcome to Watercooler Wednesday!

Here's last week's answer: 888 + 88 + 8 + 8 + 8 = 1000.

Congratulations to everyone who got the answer correct!

We're going to celebrate by talking about doughnuts today!

Do you like doughnuts? How about doughnut holes?

Do you have a favourite place where you like to buy them?

Or do you like to bake them yourself?

What flavour is your favourite?

My favourite is a chocolate cake donut covered with toasted coconut. But I have so many runners-up. I wonder if your favourite will be one of them?

☐ **#198 Date**_____

Welcome to Watercooler Wednesday!

We hope everyone who celebrates has a wonderful Easter!

Today's question may be a hard one for some people.

For Easter, if you had to choose between only eating candy, like marshmallow chicks and jellybeans, or only eating chocolate, like chocolate bunnies and chocolate eggs, which would you choose?

And for those who don't celebrate Easter, if you had to choose between only ever eating chocolate or only ever eating candy for the rest of your life, which would you choose: chocolate or candy?

As a chocoholic, this isn't even a question for me. ☺ I'm completely in for only chocolate.

☐ **#199 Date**_____

Welcome to Watercooler Wednesday!

Do you like watching TV game shows or reality TV shows?

Do you have a favourite? Why do you like it?

Have you ever been on a TV game show or reality TV show?

If not, is there one you'd like to be on?

Did you sometimes watch TV game shows as a kid when you were home sick, like I did?

Are the letters RSTLNE stuck in your head like they are for me? ☺

Are there any game shows or reality TV shows that are off the air that you would like to bring back? Any you hope will never be cancelled? Or do you have an idea for a great show?

Please share!

☐ **#200 Date**_____

Welcome to Watercooler Wednesday!

I can't believe it's the last one for April.

And speaking of things ending, are there any sayings you used to say, or heard people say, that are no longer really used anymore?

I wonder if we can come up with a long, funny list.

That would be like totally rad!

Groovy!

Gnarly!

Sweet!

MAY

☐ **#201 Date**_____

Welcome to Watercooler Wednesday!

Last week was "Far Out!" ☺ And today is May 4th so we have to celebrate Star Wars and Jane Austen.

May the Forth Be With You!

Do you have a favourite Star Wars movie?

How about a favourite character?

Are you a Star Wars collector? What do you collect?

As a kid I liked Yoda and the Ewoks. I even dressed up as Yoda once for Halloween.

May the Firth Be With You!

Do you have a favourite Jane Austen book or movie?

Do you have a favourite hero, heroine, or character?

Pride and Prejudice is at the top of my list, but all of Jane Austen's works are excellent.

And tomorrow is May 5th so Happy Cinco De Mayo!

☐ **#202 Date**_____

Welcome to Watercooler Wednesday!

I hope everyone who celebrated this past weekend had a wonderful Mother's Day!

Here are a couple of questions about Moms for fun:

1. What movie has a computer named, Mother, in it?

2. Which music group had a hit with "Mamma Mia"?

3. What do they say is the mother of invention?

Good Luck!

I'll post the answers next week. ☺

☐ **#203 Date**_____

Welcome to Watercooler Wednesday!

Here are the answers from last week:

1. Alien

2. ABBA

3. Necessity

Today's question may reflect our cultures and/or traditions, so that will be really interesting to see.

Do you take your shoes off in your home or do you leave them on?

Do you allow your guests to leave their shoes on or do they take them off, too?

We take our shoes off, and so does everyone who comes to our house.

☐ **#204 Date**_____

Welcome to Watercooler Wednesday!

What is one of your favourite places to eat fast food?

What do you like to order from them?

Do you prefer to run into the store to get your order or do you like to use the drive-through?

One of the coolest fast-food places we've been to was in Arizona.

I bet Americans can guess which fast-food place I'm talking about, even if they've never been to that exact location.

We pulled into a parking spot and ordered through a private menu. Then, the carhop came out to our car to deliver our order. All the while, we got to enjoy looking out over the beautiful mountainous landscape while we waited and then ate.

☐ **#205 Date**_____

Welcome to Watercooler Wednesday!

On the flip side of last week's question, what is one of your least favourite fast-food places?

What don't you like about their food?

Or is it something else about them that makes you avoid eating there?

Is there anything you do like about them?

Knowing the science behind it, I really detest, and refuse to eat, any food that is burnt. Hence, I avoid any place that blackens their food.

JUNE

☐ **#206 Date**_____

Welcome to Watercooler Wednesday!

Since today is the first day of June, are there any upcoming block buster movies you're looking forward to seeing?

Or any movies you've heard are in the works that you can't wait for their release?

I'm hoping there will be a good family movie at the drive-in, because it's always fun to watch movies there. ☺

☐ **#207 Date**_____

Welcome to Watercooler Wednesday!

Hopefully, this week's question is an easy

one:

If you could paint your car, or get a car in

any colour, which colour would you choose?

I think I'd pick a royal metallic blue.

☐ **#208 Date**_____

Welcome to Watercooler Wednesday!

In honour of Father's Day, here's a fun quiz:

1. What present is usually associated with Father's Day?

2. What's the name of the movie where the main character pretends to be a woman to remain close to his kids?

3. Which animal has males that get pregnant and give birth to their young?

Good luck guessing!

And Happy Father's Day!

I'll post the answers next week.

☐ **#209 Date**_____

Welcome to Watercooler Wednesday!

And welcome to summer in the Northern Hemisphere and winter in the Southern Hemisphere!

Here are the answers from last week:
1. Ties
2. Mrs. Doubtfire
3. Seahorses

Now onto today's question:
What is your favourite fruit to eat in the summer, and what is your favourite fruit to eat in the winter?

All fruit seems to taste better during the summer. For instance, strawberries smell amazing and are juicier and sweeter when in season. But I associate watermelon and cherries with summer, and clementines with winter, and hence, I tend to eat more of them during those times.

☐ **#210 Date**_____

Welcome to Watercooler Wednesday!

In honour of another school year ending, who was one of your favourite teachers? Why?

I'm lucky to have had a lot of great teachers that far outshadowed any negative ones. The teachers that really stand out were always encouraging, warm, and friendly. They truly cared and wanted the best for their students and fostered a good learning environment.

One of the best compliments I ever received was when I was getting certified to teach and an educational assistant (EA) told me she wanted me to teach her children.

JULY

☐ **#211 Date**_____

Welcome to Watercooler Wednesday!

Assuming you like trees, do you have a preference for deciduous trees (they lose their leaves) or coniferous trees (evergreens)?

I love all the variety that deciduous trees offer; some even flower. And they look pretty in the fall when they change their colours. Plus, maple trees give us maple syrup, and then there are fruit trees.

But it is nice to have green trees around all year, and you don't have to rake evergreen tree needles. Plus, they give us pinecones for decorating.

Hence, I'm glad we have both. But if I was forced to choose, I'd pick deciduous trees because of their fruit. ☺

How about you?

☐ **#212 Date**_____

Welcome to Watercooler Wednesday!

Every year I like to ask this question: Are you growing anything this year?

The last couple of years we had a garden, but this year we won't. Hopefully next year we will. But we are growing some basil, and we do have a couple of fruit trees, so we're looking forward to those later in the season.

How is your green thumb this year?

☐ **#213 Date**_____

Welcome to Watercooler Wednesday!

Do you remember a fun trip you took when you were a kid? Where did you go? What did you do? Who did you go with? What made it so memorable? Have you ever been back? Would you like to travel there again?

We took lots of family trips over the years. Sometimes we'd go as a family and other times with friends, including trips with traveling sports teams, yearly road trips, or just exciting day trips. All were so much fun and will always be treasured.

It's amazing how many unforeseen adventures can arise and how many crazy things can happen on a trip. One of our favourite ways to travel was to pick a destination and just head out not knowing where we'd stay or what we'd do along the way. I've been lucky to have revisited some of the places, but I still have many others left.

☐ **#214 Date**_____

Welcome to Watercooler Wednesday!

Here's a fun question:
What was one of your all-time favourite childhood toys?

I have so many, but I'll only mention one. It was a stuffed dog that I named, Willie, after our neighbour's dog. He was an amazing golden retriever/collie mix. I loved him and spent time with him like he was my own. Way back then my mom was scared of dogs, so we didn't have one. But after our neighbours moved, my mom came around and we got our first dog. It's hard to believe she was ever afraid of dogs; she loves them, and spoils ours. ☺

Back to toys. Did you have different toys that you loved at different ages growing up?

Do you still have any of your favourite toys?

I still have lots of mine. And it was so great to see my kids play with them and love them as much as I did.

☐ **#215 Date**_____

Welcome to Watercooler Wednesday!

Last week's question was so much fun I thought

this one would be, too. What toy on the market

right now do you think you would have loved to

play with as a kid, and wish it had existed

back then?

There are just too many dolls, learning toys,

video games, and board games that I would have

loved that I can't even list them.

AUGUST

☐ **#216 Date**_____

Welcome to Watercooler Wednesday!

Do you love photography? Are you into the latest and best cameras? Or do you just prefer to use the camera on your phone? Have you ever taken photography courses?

And while we're on the subject of pictures, have you taken any good photos lately? Maybe you've taken a photo that's quite artistic, or you've taken a photo of something you think is neat, or something you love, or maybe you just have a photo you want to share. Any photo will do, because they're all sure to be interesting and it is always so much fun to learn and experience each other's worlds.

Our youngest daughter took a photo I shared of a Bleeding Heart. I've always loved these flowers, because when I was a kid they used to be one of the first to bloom every year when the weather grew warmer.

☐ **#217 Date**_____

Welcome to Watercooler Wednesday! How is the weather where you live? Have you been through, or are you expecting, any major weather events?

It's been pretty hot here lately. I'm pretty sure this is the weather they're talking about when they say, "the dog days of summer." So, let's talk about something to cool off: swimming.

Can you swim? If yes, did you ever take lessons, or did you just learn on your own? I took some lessons and swam a lot when I was young. I can still remember playing *Ring Around the Rosie* in class to get used to going under water.

Are you a good diver? Do you like to jump into pools, or off cliffs, or off diving boards? I jumped off a diving board once in class and that was enough. ☺

Where is your favourite place to swim? Heated pools for me.

Are there games you like to play while you're swimming, such as racing, Marco Polo, volleyball, or another game?

Please share so we can all imagine having a cool time.

☐ **#218 Date**_____

Welcome to Watercooler Wednesday!

What is your favourite thing to do at the

beach?

Do you like to swim, bathe in the sun, build

sandcastles, picnic, read, or something else?

I love walking along the beach, collecting

seashells, and just taking in the fresh air,

natural sounds, and relaxing.

☐ **#219 Date**_____

Welcome to Watercooler Wednesday!

Last week's question was tons of fun! Now, let's enjoy a blast from the past.

Can you think of anything you used a lot, but now, due to technological advancements, you hardly, or never, use anymore?

I bet we could probably get quite a long list going! ☺

I'll start:

- Handles for rolling up and down car windows

- Telephones with cords or rotary dials

- VHS tapes and recorders

- Cassette tapes and recorders

- Pagers

☐ **#220 Date**_____

Welcome to Watercooler Wednesday!

I haven't mentioned this in a while, so I'll start off with this reminder: If you have any questions for Watercooler Wednesday, please message me. It's always great to get your perspective.

Now, on to today's question:

Last week we were discussing things from the past, so let's switch gears and shoot into the future.

What is something you'd like to see invented or would like to have in the future?

I would like a self-driving car.

SEPTEMBER

☐ **#221 Date**_____

Welcome to Watercooler Wednesday!

It's the beginning of a new school year! If you, your kids, or someone else in your life is headed back to school, we hope everything goes well, and it's a fantastic year!

Do you remember any of your first days of school?

Any fun memories to share?

Or perhaps you remember how you felt?

Or maybe you want to share a photo from your days in school, or of your little one(s)?

I can remember in high school, on the day before school, I would usually stay up the entire night with a mixture of nervous excitement. Hence why, I hated getting homework on the first day of school; I needed to catch up on my sleep! ☺

☐ **#222 Date**_____

Welcome to Watercooler Wednesday!

This watercooler is a place for Launchers to socialize and talk with each other about things outside of work. Hence, as always, if you have any questions you want to pose to your fellow Launchers please message me.

Now on to today's question:

What was the last thing you cooked?

Did it turn out exactly as you wanted it to?

Did you cook for yourself or for other people, as well?

And if it was for other people, did they enjoy it?

The last thing I cooked was chili, and since I've made it numerous times before, it turned out exactly as I hoped it would—thankfully. ☺

☐ **#223 Date**_____

Welcome to Watercooler Wednesday!

Do you have a favourite picture in your home?

What is it of?

Why do you love it?

Does it hold any sentimental value?

We'd love to see it if you want to share a photo of it! ☺

I have a photo of my grandparents in a fun snow globe frame. It's always nice to see them smiling at us, encouraging us, and sending us their love.

☐ **#224 Date**_____

Welcome to Watercooler Wednesday!

If you could be in any movie, which one would you want to be in?

Why would you choose that movie?

Which movie would you most definitely not want to be in? Why?

I wouldn't want to be in war or horror movies; too violent and scary.

As for a movie I'd like to be in, a period movie would be neat because then I'd get to be immersed in the history. I only hope my ability to converse as one ought in such times would properly suit. ☺

☐ **#225 Date**_____

Welcome to Watercooler Wednesday!

Have you ever taught someone something?

If so, what?

Did you enjoy the experience?

Did they learn what you were trying to teach them?

Do you remember anyone ever teaching you anything?

How did it go?

I remember as a kid, my friend and I wanted to play school, so we rounded up some kids in the neighbourhood to be our students. We tried to teach them, but it being summer, they weren't the most attentive bunch. So I suppose we learned a lesson about leading a horse to water but not being able to make it drink. ☺

OCTOBER

☐ **#226 Date**_____

Welcome to Watercooler Wednesday!

Do you like to wear jewelry?

Costume or real?

Do you have a favourite piece of jewelry?

Why do you love it?

Does it have any sentimental value?

All of my favourite jewelry has sentimental value.

We had so much fun making friendship bracelets on one of our trips.

Do you have a preference for yellow gold, white gold, rose gold, silver, platinum, stainless steel, or something else?

Do you have a favourite gemstone?

☐ **#227 Date**_____

Welcome to Watercooler Wednesday!

When you grocery shop, what is one item that you always feel good about buying?

What is one item that you always fight with yourself not to purchase?

Fruits and vegetables are always feel-good buys for me, as opposed to unnecessary junk food, emphasis on the word unnecessary. ☺

Do you shop hungry, or do you make a point to shop on a full stomach so you're not tempted to buy junk, or more than you meant to?

When you're in the store, do you like to use a cart, a basket, or just carry everything?

Or do you prefer to shop online and have your order delivered?

Do you like to do big grocery shopping orders, or do you prefer to grocery shop more often and only get a few items each time?

Do you only grocery shop at one store, or do you have several stores you like to shop at?

What grocery store is your favourite?

As you can tell from all these questions, the idea today is to talk about anything and everything to do with grocery shopping.

I worked at a grocery store for a time while in high school and university. ☺

☐ **#228 Date**_____

Welcome to Watercooler Wednesday!

Today we're going to have some fun talking
about weird things we've seen. And I know we
all may have seen some crazy stuff, but please
only share stories that would be rated G.

Have you ever witnessed something unusual or
crazy while you were shopping or out running
errands?

What happened?

For instance, have you ever seen someone
shopping in their pajamas?

Or perhaps you've witnessed one family member
carrying all the bags while the other family
members walk unencumbered in total oblivion?

I once saw three guys wearing flipflops
walking to a store on a freezing cold winter
day when there was snow on the ground. Brrr. ☺
I could not do that. I hate being cold.

☐ **#229 Date**_____

Welcome to Watercooler Wednesday!

Today we're discussing fire.

Do you enjoy sitting by a fire?

Do you like indoor fires, outdoor fires, or both?

Do you have a preference for wood-burning fires, gas fires, electric fires, or another type?

I like all different types of fires, even the ones on TV. I think they're so relaxing to watch. I love the crackling sound they make. And I think it's tons of fun to cook on them. ☺

☐ **#230 Date**_____

Welcome to Watercooler Wednesday!

Monday is Halloween!

So today's post is all about Halloween.

Do you celebrate Halloween?

Do you dress up?

Do you carve pumpkins?

Do you think we should all dress up for
Halloween?

We can post photos of ourselves, our children,
and/or our pets in costumes.

We could also post photos of decorations.

Please share your thoughts. ☺

NOVEMBER

☐ **#231 Date**_____

Welcome to Watercooler Wednesday! Hope everyone's November is off to a great start!

Shall we get some positive momentum going for this month? How about we share some good quotes or advice? It can be about anything that may inspire us.

Here are a few to get us started:

"Whether you think you can, or you think you can't – you're right." -Henry Ford

"You miss 100% of the shots you don't take." -Wayne Gretzky

"Spread love everywhere you go." -Mother Teresa

"Be the change that you wish to see in the world." -Mahatma Gandhi

☐ **#232 Date**_____

Welcome to Watercooler Wednesday!

The new year will be here in less than two months.

Are you looking forward to the new year?

Or would you rather put on the brakes?

I need the brakes put on because there's so much I still need to do this year.

☐ **#233 Date**_____

Welcome to Watercooler Wednesday!

If you could plan a holiday to anywhere in the world, where would you go?

Why do you want to go there?

Who would you take with you?

What things would you want to see while you were there?

What exciting things would you wish to explore or experience?

Or would you prefer to just sit back, relax, and be catered to?

Since it's November, I would choose a warm location and take my family somewhere we've never been before. Then we could relax, but also explore the area and learn as much about it as possible.

☐ **#234 Date**_____

Welcome to Watercooler Wednesday!

Happy Thanksgiving to those celebrating in the United States!

Let's all pretend we're enjoying a delicious Thanksgiving Day meal, or if you don't celebrate Thanksgiving, the dinner of another big celebration that has all the food you love.

With that in mind, please answer today's question:

Would you rather be the one who cooks the food for everyone, or the one who has to wash all the dirty dishes?

My mom is a fabulous cook, so if she's cooking, I'd choose to do the dishes. But if I bake dessert, then it would be great to have someone else clean up everything.

How about you?

Chef or kitchen clean-up crew?

☐ **#235 Date**_____

Welcome to Watercooler Wednesday!

And the last Watercooler Wednesday of November!

Today we're talking about music.

Do you usually have music playing or do you only listen to music at certain times and in certain places?

Do you have certain music you play for certain occasions? For example, the radio while working, rock bands while you clean, and classical music when you're relaxing?

I always drive with music on and probably have music on more often than not. I usually just listen to whatever I'm in the mood for at the time. ☺

DECEMBER

☐ **#236 Date**_____

Welcome to Watercooler Wednesday!

Have you ever been to a Santa Claus Parade?

Do you like to attend them or do you prefer to watch them on TV?

Have you seen any amazing floats?

Or heard any great music at them?

I always look forward to hearing bagpipes.
It's one of the only times I get to hear them played live.

If you don't have Santa Claus parades where you live, do you enjoy other parades or processions?

Please share. ☺

☐ **#237 Date**_____

Welcome to Watercooler Wednesday!

Here's a fun question:

Outside of work, what is one thing you like to enjoy right now?

Eating Christmas goodies may be high on everyone's list. ☺

But it could be something you do every day, or something you look forward to doing on the weekend, or maybe it's a special event you have planned for this month.

I love to watch Christmas movies, listen to Christmas music, and read Christmas books at this time of year. All things Christmas! ☺

☐ **#238 Date**_____

Welcome to Watercooler Wednesday!

The end of the year is almost here, so let's take some time to look back at this year.

What is one delicious new food you discovered this year?

Were there any tasty new drinks you discovered?

I discovered a new to me tea. It's a blend of pomegranate and raspberry flavours, and it quickly became a favourite. It smells fantastic! I'd been drinking it hot, but thanks to our oldest daughter's experiments, it's also excellent as iced tea. ☺ And now I can't wait until summer to really enjoy it as a cold drink outside.

☐ **#239 Date**_____

Welcome to Watercooler Wednesday!

Let's take a look back at this year.

A lot happened!

What is something you think will make it into
the history books when they write about this
year?

It could be a political event, a medical
advancement, something from pop culture, a
natural disaster, or something else.

Sometimes I wonder how people in the future
are going to sift through all of our history,
because unlike the dark ages, in this age of
information we sure do produce and store a lot
of intel.

☐ **#240 Date**_____

Welcome to the last Watercooler Wednesday of
the year! Thank you to everyone who
participated in Welcome To Watercooler
Wednesday and made this a fun year!

Hopefully we will all enjoy some wonderful
holiday time and then we'll be back in the new
year refreshed and ready to have even more
fun!

Since this is our last topic of the year, and
we've been reflecting on this past year, let's
leave on the most positive note. Let's spread
some good cheer and build each other up!

Can you think of anyone at TestLauncher you'd
like to thank for helping you? Or someone who
made a difference in your work life this year?
It can be anything from someone who put a
smile on your face, to someone who said
something encouraging to you. Basically,
anything someone did that impacted you in a
good way.

My hope is that each of you will be able to
compliment at least one other person until
everyone has a nice note about them.

You are all important and special to
TestLauncher, and very much appreciated! And
hopefully today we can show each other that.

Spread some joy!

Lift each other up!

And show your appreciation for your
TestLauncher teammates!

YEAR 5

JANUARY

☐ **#241 Date**_____

Welcome to the first Watercooler Wednesday of the new year!

As a new year stretches before us full of endless possibilities what are you looking forward to?

Do you have any special events coming up this year!

Have you made any New Year's resolutions?

What one word, or phrase, would you choose to strive to live up to this year?

I don't make New Year's resolutions, but I do like the idea of having a word, or phrase, to focus on during the year.

☐ **#242 Date**_____

Welcome to Watercooler Wednesday!

Here's a fun puzzle! Can you figure it out?

Iguana Fox
Yak Otter Unicorn
Cat Alligator Narwhale
Rabbit Elephant Alligator Dear
Turtle Hippo Iguana Skunk
Cat Otter Mouse Mouse Elephant Narwhale Turtle
Walrus Iguana Turtle Hippo
Alligator
Hippo Elephant Alligator Rabbit Turtle
Iguana Fox
Narwhale Otter Turtle
Iguana
Walrus Iguana Lion Lion
Turtle Elephant Lion Lion
Elephant Vulture Elephant Rabbit Yak
Otter Narwhale Elephant
Narwhale Elephant Xerus Turtle
Walrus Elephant Elephant Kangaroo

Good luck! I'll share the answer next week.

☐ **#243 Date**_____

Welcome to Watercooler Wednesday!

Last week was fun!

A lot of you solved the puzzle! Way to go!
That was awesome!

The answer involved the first letter of each
word.

IF YOU CAN READ THIS
COMMENT WITH A HEART
IF NOT
I WILL TELL EVERYONE NEXT WEEK

Today I want to ask you how you would describe
someone who would be a good fit at
TestLauncher?

What character traits, personality, or skill
sets do you think someone needs to possess in
order to successfully work at TestLauncher?

What do you think would be a definite 'do not
apply'?

☐ **#244 Date**_____

Welcome to Watercooler Wednesday!

If you could make any wild animal tame and have it as a pet, which wild animal would you choose? And why?

This is a super hard question. There are so many animals that I wish were domesticated.

But foxes sure are cute, they are part of the dog family, and as a kid I did love the Disney movie, The Fox and The Hound.

Hmmm.

What is your answer to this question?

Go wild!

☐ **#245 Date**_____

Welcome to Watercooler Wednesday!

What is your favourite food to eat for breakfast?

Do you gravitate toward cereal, bagels, pancakes, waffles, fruit, pastries, toast, ham, sausage, muffins, eggs, croissants, oatmeal, or something else?

What is your favourite drink to enjoy at breakfast?

Do you start your day with water, coffee, tea, milk, juice, smoothies, or something else?

I don't really have a favourite breakfast food, but I must have my hot chocolate or chocolate milk in the morning.

FEBRUARY

☐ **#246 Date**_____

Welcome to Watercooler Wednesday!

What is your favourite food to snack on?

Do you tend to snack on healthy food, or do you prefer to satisfy your sweet tooth at snack time?

I try to snack on healthy food, like grapes or bananas. They're quick and easy, and they taste great. I also tend to go for the same food for a while and then change to something else.

Do you snack at the same time(s) every day or do you change it up every day? Or do you refuse to snack between meals?

I snack at roughly the same times every day.

Please tell us all about your snack attacks. ☺

☐ **#247 Date**_____

Welcome to Watercooler Wednesday!

Happy Valentine's Day!

Do you decorate for Valentine's Day?

We do, although not nearly as much as other occasions, like Christmas, Easter, Halloween, or for parties. ☺

What kind of decorations do you display?

We use anything that makes us smile, from window clings to flowers.

Do you keep your decorations and reuse them year after year, or do you throw them away and buy new ones every year?

We reuse ours. And adding to our collection is always so much fun!

☐ **#248 Date**_____

Welcome to Watercooler Wednesday!

Have you ever had a really bad haircut? One where you wanted to wear a hat? Or stay inside until your hair grew back?

Or perhaps you were lucky and had a really great haircut, and now have a photo to share?

I remember as a kid, my mom was cutting my hair as usual, but for some reason she couldn't get my hair straight and so she kept cutting. You can imagine my surprise when I saw my long hair had become short!

Dogs always look so cute after they come home from the groomers. And most groomers dress them up with bandanas, or hair clips, or something else really adorable. ☺

Do you take your pet(s) to the groomers? Or do you enjoy doing that yourself?

Any photos or stories to share?

☐ **#249 Date**_____

Welcome to Watercooler Wednesday!

Do you have a favourite book?
How many times have you read it?
Why do you love it so much?
Do you think others will like it?

I can't wait to read your recommendations!

And I apologize, but to choose between every book I've enjoyed to determine a favourite is literally impossible for me. ☺

Hence, I will restrict myself to only three classic novels. One would be, Our Mutual Friend by Charles Dickens, because the twist in this book was fabulous, and Dickens always sees to it that the bad guys get their just desserts, while the good characters get their happily ever after. Also, Pride and Prejudice by Jane Austen, because it is most entertaining and provides a fun insight into human nature. And then there's The Hobbit by J.R.R. Tolkien, which is an epic adventure.

☐ **#250 Date**_____

Welcome to Watercooler Wednesday!

Aside from being in an airplane, what is the highest altitude you've ever been to?

Have you climbed any tall mountains?

Or do you live at a high altitude?

The highest I've ever gone up in an elevator is to the top of the CN Tower in Toronto, Ontario, Canada. On foot, it would be Camelback Mountain in Phoenix, Arizona, USA. And in a vehicle, Sedona, Arizona, USA to spots like the Seven Sacred Pools. Although, Pena Palace in Sintra, Portugal was also way up in the sky.

MARCH

☐ **#251 Date**_____

Welcome to Watercooler Wednesday!

What is your favourite cut flower to buy or receive? Why?

And what is your least favourite cut flower to buy or receive? Why?

I love carnations. I love how they smell and that they last for two weeks. Then there are roses, which I can dry and keep for a long time. I still have the rose from my first date with Jason. But daisies are pretty, too. And gladioli are striking. And I'm sure you will remind me of even more flowers I love to give and receive. ☺

As for flowers I don't like, I'm not sure if there are any. But maybe you can help me with that, too. Perhaps there are some really stinky flowers I don't know about and should avoid? ☺

☐ **#252 Date**_____

Welcome to Watercooler Wednesday!

The amount of daylight hours rise from winter through spring, so I thought we could talk about sunshine today.

When it's sunny outside, do you like to be in the sun or do you prefer to be in the shade?

When you want to block the sun, what are your preferred methods? For instance, are you a fan of sunscreen? Do you wear a hat? Do you don sunglasses? Or do you use an umbrella, wear clothes that cover your skin, or some other method?

Please share, and grace us with your sunny disposition. ☺

I like to feel the sun on my skin, but I hate to burn and try to always avoid that. I usually find the shade if it's extremely hot outside. Otherwise, more often than not, I wear a hat and sunglasses.

☐ **#253 Date**_____

Welcome to Watercooler Wednesday!

March Break, aka Spring Break, is upon us.

Do the kids where you live get this week off from school?

Did you get March Break when you were a kid?

Here the elementary and high school students get March Break, but university and college students have Reading Week in February.

What is, was, or would be, your favourite thing to do on March Break or Reading Week?

A lot of people go on vacation, are you planning a trip?

I remember one March Break when we were kids, the weather was so hot it was like having a taste of summer vacation. We spent the entire week outside playing in shorts and t-shirts, and it was so much fun!

In university though, Reading Week was fun, but also a great time to catch up and get ahead on schoolwork.

☐ **#254 Date**_____

Welcome to Watercooler Wednesday!

And welcome to spring in the Northern Hemisphere and fall in the Southern Hemisphere!

What signs of spring are visible where you live?

And for those in fall, how can you tell a change has occurred?

I can't wait for the smell of fresh cut grass, magnolias, lilacs, and hyacinths. ☺

Have you noticed any new or returning backyard critters?

And speaking of creatures who like to make themselves comfortable, where is your favourite spot to sit and relax?

Do you have a favourite living room chair? Or a favourite spot on the sofa?

Do you like to recline and put your feet up, or do you prefer to curl up in your favourite spot?

And when you're outside, do you have a favourite outdoor bench, chair, swing, or lounger you love to relax on?

☐ **#255 Date**_____

Welcome to Watercooler Wednesday!

And the last week of March, which is the name
of our topic for this week.

Were you ever in a **march**ing band?

Did you ever take part in a **march**?

Do you feel as if time just **march**es on?

You can either answer any, or all, of the
above questions, or make up your own question
with the root word, march. ☺

I was never in a marching band. I've never
marched for, or against, anything. But yes, I
do feel as if time does march on.

APRIL

☐ **#256 Date**_____

Welcome to Watercooler Wednesday!

In honour of National Siblings Day, let's talk about our families.

Were you an only child or did you have brothers and/or sisters?

If you had siblings, how many did you have, and where did you fall in the birth order?

I've been so blessed with a close, loving family. I have an older brother who's always been my best friend, along with my parents. And a funny coincidence with birthdays: my older brother and our eldest daughter have birthdays in the same month only a few days apart, while our youngest daughter and myself have birthdays in the same month only a few days apart. Talk about history repeating itself. ☺

☐ **#257 Date**_____

Welcome to Watercooler Wednesday!

I 'hop' you're ready for some Easter Trivia!

1. What is a baby rabbit called? Hint: It's not
   a bunny.

2. In the Disney movie, Bambi, what is the name
   of Bambi's rabbit friend?

3. In what country were Fabergé eggs made?

4. What country is known for its elaborately
   decorated Easter Eggs called Pysanky?

I'll post the answers next week.

Good Luck! And Happy Easter!

☐ **#258 Date**_____

Welcome to Watercooler Wednesday! I hope those who celebrated enjoyed a fabulous Easter! As promised here are the answers from last week:

1. Kit
2. Thumper
3. Russia
4. Ukraine

Speaking of amazing works of art like the Fabergé eggs and Pysanky, are there any great pieces of art from history that you adore? For instance, do you love any works from Leonardo da Vinci, Vincent van Gogh, Pablo Picasso, Michelangelo, Monet, Rembrandt, etc.

Or do you prefer more modern artists and their work?

I have so much respect for Mouth & Foot Painting Artists. They create incredible art despite not having the use of their hands. But it's more than that, they're inspirational since they don't allow their circumstances to hinder them.

☐ **#259 Date**_____

Welcome to Watercooler Wednesday!

Earth Day is coming up. Are you doing anything to mark Earth Day? For instance, will you be shutting off your lights for a certain amount of time?

What is something easy, such as not littering, that you wish people would do to help the earth?

And speaking of the earth, are there any endangered species that you're really concerned about?

What are some things we can do to help those animals?

I love spending Earth Day outside in nature, gardening, and planting if the weather permits.

And remember these words by Dr. Jane Goodall, **"What you do makes a difference, and you have to decide what kind of difference you want to make."**

☐ **#260 Date**_____

Welcome to Watercooler Wednesday!

Let's talk about music!

Who played at the first concert you ever attended?

What was the last concert you went to?

Do you still like going to concerts?

If you could see anyone live, whose concert would you like to attend?

I've been to my fair share of concerts, but one that always stands out was a Paul Anka concert in Niagara Falls. I love oldies music, and one year on Valentine's Day, Jason and I renewed our wedding vows at a private event with other couples. After the ceremony we all had dinner with a special guest appearance from Paul Anka. He gave every couple a gift. Then, we got to watch his concert, which was terrific.

MAY

☐ **#261 Date**_____

Welcome to Watercooler Wednesday! Planting season is upon us.

What are your favourite flowers to plant outdoors, and what are your least favourite ones?

And if you don't plant any flowers, which ones do you love that other people plant? And which ones don't you like to see planted?

I like planting yellow marigolds. They're supposed to ward off mosquitoes and they last all the way to Halloween. Hence, they're beautiful for three seasons.

Do you overwinter any plants and then put them outside when the weather warms up? We do.

☐ **#262 Date**_____

Welcome to Watercooler Wednesday! Happy Mother's Day!

What is one story about you that your mother or mother figure holds dear?

It could be something she thought was hilarious, or something that touched her heart.

And on the flip side, what is one story you hold dear about your mother or mother figure?

Please share.

My mom and I both remember when I was two and she would try her hardest to be as quiet as she could while she got ready for work in the morning, but despite how quiet she was, I would always wake up and join her in the bathroom. She would sit me on the counter, and I would watch her put on her make-up and do her hair. She was always baffled at my internal alarm clock, because on the days she didn't go into work I would sleep in.

☐ **#263 Date**_____

Welcome to Watercooler Wednesday!

In Canada, we celebrate Queen Victoria's birthday on May 24th.

Canadians refer to this holiday as the May Two-Four, and it's the official weekend that kicks off summer.

Canadians, do you have any exciting plans on the horizon?

And for those in other countries, how do you kick off your summer season?

There are always lots of fireworks here. ☺

☐ **#264 Date**_____

Welcome to Watercooler Wednesday!

We've talked before about what we think is the best invention ever. Now let's see if we can determine what the worst invention was. Or the most useless one.

This should be fun!

I think it best if I don't answer this question in this book. Hence, I'll just hint at my answer by saying that there was a product that was once so popular, and yet so common, it must have had the best marketing ever to sell it. I guess people thought it was funny. But I can't believe they actually spent money on it. Good thing it wasn't really that expensive. Although it did make the creator a lot of money, so if we look at it from the creator's perspective it wasn't useless at all.

☐ **#265 Date**_____

Welcome to Watercooler Wednesday!

What is one song you love to hear when you're at a party?

Anything familiar that's upbeat is a welcome choice for me.

When you hear 'your song' do you get up and dance?

Do you sing along with it?

Or are you just happy to bop your head, stomp your foot, or tap your fingers?

Are there any songs you request because they're hardly played?

If you had to sing karaoke, what song would you choose to sing? Would you sing a solo, or do you prefer to sing duets or in a group? Or is there absolutely no way you would sing karaoke?

JUNE

☐ **#266 Date**_____

Welcome to Watercooler Wednesday!

Have you ever been on a cruise? Where did your cruise ship take you? Did you enjoy your adventure?

If you've never been on a cruise, or if you want to cruise again, where would you go?

I am always in awe at how huge cruise ships are and how many activities are onboard.

Have you ever been on a shorter river cruise or a cruise on a lake? I love those, and lots of cities have dinner cruises or cruises especially for tourists that teach all sorts of interesting local facts.

☐ **#267 Date**_____

Welcome to Watercooler Wednesday!

Happy Father's Day!

What is one story your father or father figure holds dear about you?

It could be something he thought was hilarious, or something that touched his heart.

And on the flip side, what is one story you hold dear about your father or father figure?

Once when I was a teenager my dad dressed up as a priest for Halloween. My parents are ballroom dancers and hence were at an event dancing when this woman yelled at him, because she didn't think he was conducting himself as a priest should. She really tore into him in front of everyone. My mom tried so hard to convince the woman my dad was her husband and not really a priest, but the woman didn't believe her. Finally, a board member stepped in to vouch for them. LOL

☐ **#268 Date**_____

Welcome to Watercooler Wednesday! And welcome
to summer in the Northern Hemisphere and
winter in the Southern Hemisphere!

What is one thing you're really looking
forward to this season?

And what is something you're really not
looking forward to this season?

I'm looking forward to spending lots of time
outside this summer. But the bugs and creepy
crawly things are what I dislike the most
about this time of year.

Do you like snakes? How about reptiles? Do you
pick them up? For those who don't like them,
have you ever touched them? I don't care for
them enough to have them as a pet, but I do
think lizards look neat when they walk.

Do you like any creatures that most people
don't? I like frogs and toads. But I'm not
sure if that counts.

☐ **#269 Date**_____

Welcome to Watercooler Wednesday!

What is your favourite mode of transportation?

Do you enjoy traveling by car, plane, train,

scooter, skateboard, helicopter, or by

jogging, canoeing, or some other mode of

transportation?

I love being on the water. Next is probably

walking, because I love to take in all the

sights and sounds.

☐ **#270 Date**_____

Welcome to Watercooler Wednesday!

Here's a fun question where hopefully we can learn from each other's mistakes or at least get a laugh out of them! ☺

What is something you've done, that you will never do again?

What made it such a terrible experience?

Even though you'd never do it again, are you glad you did do it?

For me, back roading with a *new* driver who had us teetering on the edge of cliffs, several times, is not something I'm eager to repeat. The views were beautiful though. And in the driver's defence, we did live to tell about it. ☺ Also, my kids won't be going on a speed boat any time soon to go looking for dolphins or whales. They're not sure how we didn't die, especially when our driver ended the adventure by speeding toward a bridge and then turning sharply just before we hit it.

JULY

☐ **#271 Date**_____

Welcome to Watercooler Wednesday!

Happy Canada Day! And Happy 4th of July!

Do you like fireworks?

Do you have any favourite ones?

How about your pets? Do they have issues with all the noise, or do they not seem to care?

Do you like to watch professional fireworks, or do you like to set off your own?

As a kid I have great memories of our family setting off fireworks with another family. Now we enjoy the beautiful fireworks in Niagara Falls. They're lit everyday throughout the summer, and at certain times during the year, too. I especially like the sparkly ones.

☐ **#272 Date**_____

Welcome to Watercooler Wednesday!

What is your favourite wildflower?

What is your least favourite wildflower?

I love wildflowers because they're hardy and pretty.

Hmmm, there aren't many I don't like except for ones that are dangerous like giant hogweed and wild parsnip which can burn your skin.

Do you like dandelions?

Would you consider them a weed or a wildflower?

Do you eat them or use them in tea?

☐ **#273 Date**_____

Welcome to Watercooler Wednesday!

Here's a fun topic: Collections.

What do you like to collect?

What did you like to collect when you were a kid?

Is there something new you'd like to collect?

We like to collect Christmas ornaments. Every year we pick out a special one that has significant meaning. And it's always extra special to add homemade ones to our collection, too.

Happy Christmas in July! ☺

☐ **#274 Date**_____

Welcome to Watercooler Wednesday!

Do you like to BBQ? What is your favourite food to BBQ?

Do you have a favourite BBQ? For instance, do you have a preference for propane BBQs over charcoal ones?

If you don't have a BBQ, do like to eat barbequed food?

What is your favourite barbequed food?

Barbequing food does seem to change the taste of the food. For instance, hotdogs taste so much better barbequed than boiled. And my dad makes these amazing chicken wings on the BBQ.

My least favourite barbequed food is corn on the cob. I'd much rather have it boiled.

Your turn to make us hungry. ☺

☐ **#275 Date**_____

Welcome to Watercooler Wednesday!

When you go swimming, do you dive right in or do you need time to acclimatize yourself to the water?

I take my sweet time getting in. And the colder the water, the longer it takes. ☺ Jason however, jumps right in.

Do you have a favourite swim stroke, such as the butterfly stroke or the backstroke?

Or do you prefer to lie on a pool lounger and just float around the pool?

Does your pet like to swim?

Our collies aren't fans of swimming, but they absolutely love playing with the hose and sprinklers.

AUGUST

☐ **#276 Date**_____

Welcome to Watercooler Wednesday!

Time for some fun rapid-fire questions.

Would you rather be on the water paddling a boat or sitting and relaxing on the dock? -On the water, then relax later.

Would you rather be swimming in a pool or reading on a poolside lounger? -Depends on the day, but swim, then read later.

Would you rather play with water balloons or run a three-legged race? -Water balloons.

Would you rather sit by a fire and make s'mores or watch firecrackers? -That's a hard one. I'd rather sit by the fire while watching firecrackers.

Would you rather go camping or stay at a hotel? -Hotel.

I can't wait to see what everyone's preferences are. And if you have any fun rapid fire *would you rather* questions to add, please do so and we'll answer yours, as well.

☐ **#277 Date**_____

Welcome to Watercooler Wednesday!

Have you come across any gross, scary, interesting, or cute insects or creatures lately?

Please share anything you want, even if it's a child hanging upside down from the monkey bars looking like a sloth. ☺

Thankfully we didn't touch the beautiful, fluffy white Hickory Tussock Moth Caterpillar we found, because even though it may look pretty it's poisonous and would be like touching poison ivy. We've also seen some stick bugs this year which are really neat!

☐ **#278 Date**_____

Welcome to Watercooler Wednesday!

What sounds, smells, tastes, and/or textures

do you associate with this time of the year?

It's summer here, so the sound of birds

chirping, the smell of pool chlorine, the

taste of sweet, juicy cherries, and the feel

of warm rocks scream summer.

☐ **#279 Date**_____

Welcome to Watercooler Wednesday!

Here are some more fun rapid fire *would you rather* questions:

Would you rather drink iced coffee or iced tea? -Iced tea.

Would you rather live in the Arctic during the summer when they have only sunlight all day and night, or live in the Antarctic during the same time period when they only have darkness? -The Arctic.

Would you rather eat only barbequed food during summer or eat only cold, uncooked food during summer? -Cold, uncooked food.

Would you rather swim in a pool or sit in a hot tub? -Hot tub.

Would you rather live in a tree house for the summer or in a tent? -A tent.

Would you rather eat a picnic on a blanket on the ground or at a picnic table? -Picnic table.

☐ **#280 Date**_____

Welcome to Watercooler Wednesday!

The Labour Day long weekend is coming up.

Since we all live in different places and lead
such wonderful lives, today's question is sure
to bring us various answers that should
energize us all.

What are you excited about right now?

It may be an upcoming event, a daytrip you
just took, a book you're reading, or just
having a minute to sit and relax.

Please share.

I'm excited about getting to pick apples soon.

SEPTEMBER

☐ **#281 Date**_____

Welcome to Watercooler Wednesday!

A new school year is upon us.

Good luck to everyone going back!

Do you like back-to-school shopping?

Did you like it as a kid?

What things do you especially like to shop for?

What things did you love to shop for as a kid?

What things do you hate to shop for?

Or did you hate to shop for as a kid?

I love shopping for school supplies, aka office supplies! Pens, notebooks, etc. ☺

☐ **#282 Date**_____

Welcome to Watercooler Wednesday!

It's the beginning of September when people tend to spend more time indoors. So let's bring the conversation inside.

What is your oldest indoor plant?

How long have you had your plant?

Does it hold any special memories? For example, did you get your plant when you moved into your home, or did you inherit your plant from a loved one?

We'd love to see photos.

We recently lost a fifteen year old saguaro, so now our oldest four plants were part of a basket we received from my parents when our youngest was born.

What is your newest indoor plant?

One of our newest indoor plants is a snake plant. But I've added quite a few plants lately, like a Christmas cactus. ☺

☐ **#283 Date**_____

Welcome to Watercooler Wednesday!

Do you like to wear slippers? What are your favourite kinds of slippers?

We don't normally wear slippers, but my parents always do.

If you don't wear slippers, do you prefer to walk around your house in socks, bare feet, or keep your shoes on?

Socks or bare feet.

Do your pets like slippers?

Our dogs both loved slippers and shoes. When they were puppies we always had to remember to put them away. ☺ It's such a relief when puppies are trained and outgrow that stage. And finding your dog sleeping on your shoes is just so cute! ☺

☐ **#284 Date**_____

Welcome to Watercooler Wednesday!

Have you ever been the recipient of a surprise? Perhaps someone threw you a surprise party or surprised you with something?

Have you ever surprised someone?

How did you pull it off?

If not, and you could surprise someone, who would you surprise? Why? And how would you do it?

Please share. ☺

I love throwing surprise parties. We've successfully surprised both of my parents with parties over the years. One time, when we were surprising my dad—he was so funny—he opened the door to the surprise party, then shut it and bolted to tell my mom, but of course she already knew. ☺ I did have a surprise fail once though, when someone who was in on the surprise party didn't keep the secret.

☐ **#285 Date**_____

Welcome to Watercooler Wednesday and the beginning of fall/spring!

Have you ever heard of woolly mammoth caterpillars? We are apparently supposed to be able to predict how long and cold winter will be, and the amount of snowfall we will get depending on how they look.

Do you think their appearance does correctly predict winter weather?

Do you know of any other ways that people have or still use to predict things like the weather?

There's an old saying that roots back to the bible, **"Red sky at night, sailor's delight. Red sky in morning, sailor's warning."**

OCTOBER

☐ **#286 Date**_____

Welcome to Watercooler Wednesday!

What is your favourite indoor flowering plant to buy or receive?

I think I will pick orchids.

There are so many colours and they last a long time.

And if you're lucky, they can even rebloom.

What is your least favourite indoor flowering plant to buy or receive?

Although I love how they look, I'll say Easter Lilies because their fragrance is very strong. But, I could always just plant them outside, so problem solved.

☐ **#287 Date**_____

Welcome to Watercooler Wednesday! Happy Thanksgiving for those who celebrated in Canada!

Have you ever broken a turkey's wishbone at Thanksgiving?

If you get the larger half you're supposed to get your wish. Did you?

I have had fun doing that, but I can't remember if my wishes ever came true.

What other things do you know of that are supposed to bestow good luck on a person?

One that is always fun is blowing the seeds off of dandelions. And I'm sure we can come up with quite a list. ☺

☐ **#288 Date**_____

Welcome to Watercooler Wednesday!

I hope this question doesn't drive anyone crazy. ☺

Do you know how to drive?

What vehicles are you licensed to drive?

When did you learn to drive?

Who taught you?

And if you don't drive, do you drive anything, like go-carts, bumper boats, etc.?

I didn't waste any time; on my sixteenth birthday I wrote my driver's test and got my learner's permit that day. Then I went to a great driving school that I always recommend.

☐ **#289 Date**_____

Welcome to Watercooler Wednesday!

What is the weirdest coincidence that has ever

happened to you or someone you know?

While driving home one night, I told Jason

about a show I had watched with our daughters

a couple weeks before. In the show, one of the

main characters had stopped her car at a stop

sign and a deer ran into her car. As soon as I

finished telling the story, an owl flew into

our windshield and hit it directly in front of

me!

☐ #290 Date_____

Welcome to Watercooler Wednesday!

Happy Halloween!

Do you like horror movies?

Which horror movie is your favourite?

I watched some horror movies as a kid and they freaked me out!

I have a very active, or more accurately, an over-active imagination.

Hence, I don't watch them anymore and I will be stepping aside today and asking our horror movie lovers to keep the conversation going.

Have fun scaring yourselves! ☺

I'll see you in November! Unless there's a zombie apocalypse.

NOVEMBER

☐ **#291 Date**_____

Welcome to Watercooler Wednesday!

There are only two months left in this year.

Hence, today's question allows us to dream and

wish for the future.

What is something you really want to do, but

haven't had the opportunity to do it yet?

I cannot wait to cross-country ski.

☐ **#292 Date**_____

Welcome to Watercooler Wednesday!

When you have a life-altering decision to make, what is your process?

For instance, do you talk it over with people, write a pros and cons list, sit in solitude to think, sleep on it, flip a coin, or some other method, or combination of methods?

I do a combination of methods, but they all involve talking it over with trusted people who I know will give me their honest opinion, which I value. Plus, I pray about it. Then, if I can, I wait at least one day before going ahead with any major decisions.

How about you?

Care to share any of your big, life-altering decisions that you had to make?

Are you happy with what you decided?

☐ **#293 Date**_____

Welcome to Watercooler Wednesday!

Imagine you had a bad day, what would you do
to make yourself feel better?

There are so many ways to try and get out of a
bad mood, like exercising to get those happy
endorphins going or watching something funny
to make yourself laugh.

Just smiling for no reason can change your
brain chemistry.

And of course, any excuse for chocolate,
right? ☺

☐ **#294 Date**_____

Welcome to Watercooler Wednesday!

Happy American Thanksgiving to everyone celebrating!

In the spirit of giving and being thankful, have you ever been the recipient of a random act of kindness?

Have you ever performed a random act of kindness?

Please share your stories.

I love everything about random acts of kindness. I love performing them, and I am always so thankful to receive them. They really do make our world a better place. And even the tiniest acts can greatly impact people in unimaginable ways. For instance, there was a man on a beach in California who saw my daughters looking for shells and gave them a sand dollar. How sweet was that? ☺

☐ **#295 Date**_____

Welcome to Watercooler Wednesday!

We're ending November with a tough question!

If you were able to travel through time but you could only go one way, either into the future or into the past, which way would you choose?

Dilemmas! Dilemmas! ☺

But how could I pass up going back in time to meet Jesus?

DECEMBER

☐ **#296 Date**_____

Welcome to Watercooler Wednesday!

Did you have an advent calendar as a kid?

What do you remember getting inside yours?

Did you follow the rules and only open one door a day?

Do you still have an advent calendar now?

If you do, or even if you don't, what things do you like, or would you like, to get in your advent calendar? Chocolate, tea, socks, or something else?

I always appreciate chocolate, but one of my favourite advent calendars was one that had a necklace and a bracelet with Christmas charms.

☐ **#297 Date**_____

Welcome to Watercooler Wednesday!

What kind of holiday shopper are you?

Do you shop for holiday presents a long time in advance, or are you a last-minute shopper?

Do you make lists, or do you roam through stores until you find that perfect gift?

I make lists, and I shop so far in advance for every occasion that if I wrap the presents when I buy them, I can usually forget what I bought and be surprised along with the recipient. ☺

☐ **#298 Date**_____

Welcome to Watercooler Wednesday! And Welcome to winter in the Northern Hemisphere and summer in the Southern Hemisphere!

Where you live, do animals, or people, migrate?

Which animals migrate?

Where do they go?

Do any animals hibernate?

Which ones?

We have lots of animals that go somewhere warmer during the winter months. And a lot of people, called Snowbirds, do so, as well.

Monarch butterflies go down to Mexico. And seagulls don't usually stick around.

Although there are a lot of animals that don't migrate, like some geese and chickadees.

☐ **#299 Date**_____

Welcome to Watercooler Wednesday!

Let's talk about everything and anything to do
with holiday decorations!

Have you seen any incredible decorations?

Do you decorate for the holidays? Do you go
overboard, or do you only do the bare minimum?

Do you decorate your entire house, or just
certain rooms?

Do you decorate with other people, or do you
do all the decorating yourself?

What is your favourite decoration?

When do you start decorating?

When do you take your decorations down?

We definitely decorate for the holidays. And
we've seen some fantastic decorations, like
giant outdoor Rudolph and Clarice reindeer the
size of a house, homes completely covered in
lights, entire front yards full of
decorations, etc.

I absolutely love seeing Christmas lights and
think there should be some sort of award
program for the people who truly make their
homes magical!

☐ **#300 Date**_____

Welcome to the last Watercooler Wednesday of the year!

What are some fabulous things that happened to you this past year?

What are some exciting things you're looking forward to in the new year?

Where will you be spending New Year's Eve?

Who will you be ringing the new year in with?

Jason and I want to thank you for making TestLauncher awesome this year! We truly have incredible people here at TestLauncher that we are so proud of! Everyone worked hard this year and we know next year will be just as great! We hope you enjoy your holidays and wish you all the very best, today and always!

Happy New Year from our family to yours!

Dear Reader,

I hope you enjoyed **GET TO KNOW A CEO!**

I would love to hear how you put Watercooler Wednesday to good use!

If you would like us to implement Welcome To Watercooler Wednesday for you, please reach out to us at:
www.WelcomeToWatercoolerWednesday.com

If you wish to connect, please do so at any, or all, of the following:

www.LilacLanePublishing.com

www.TestLauncher.com

www.EvaMariaHamilton.com

I look forward to meeting you, and staying in touch!

Sincerely,

Eva Maria Hamilton

About the Author

Eva Maria Hamilton spent years studying people from all different areas of academia. As an advocate for lifelong learning, Eva studied in both Canada and the United States, earning a Diploma in Human Resources Management, a Bachelor of Arts Degree in Psychology, an Honours Bachelor of Arts Degree in History, and a Master of Science in Education.

Eva Maria Hamilton is committed to being a modern-day Renaissance woman. She homeschooled her oldest daughter, Michelina, who began university at age sixteen, and still homeschools her youngest daughter, Angelina, along with their two collies, Daisy and Glory, while working as an author and publisher, and acting as Co-CEO in her Co-Founded business, TestLauncher, with her husband, Jason.

Eva Maria Hamilton has always had a deep-seated love of entrepreneurship. Her company, TestLauncher, was featured in The Financial Times for winning The Americas' Fastest Growing Companies 2024 award.

Eva Maria Hamilton is the author of many novels, including Highland Hearts, a Love Inspired Historical novel published by Harlequin.

Her novel, Highland Hearts:

- **Won 2nd Place in the Heart of Excellence, Reader's Choice Contest - Historical Romance Category**

- **Won 2nd Place in the Heart of Excellence, Reader's Choice Contest - Inspirational/Traditional Romance Category**

- Was an **Inspirational Series Finalist in the 2013 Gayle Wilson Award of Excellence**

Eva Maria Hamilton is also the owner of Lilac Lane Publishing, where she has published a series of Jane Austen Colouring & Activity Books.

Her book, The Ultimate Collection of Jane Austen's Colouring and Activity Books: With More Than 240 Activities And Over 250 Illustrations from 1875-1906:

- **Won the 2024 International Impact Book Awards**

www.ingramcontent.com/pod-product-compliance
Lightning Source LLC
Chambersburg PA
CBHW061927190326
41458CB00009B/2678